"Andrew Ramer . . . seer, poet, storyteller . . . the man with the moon over his shoulder . . . He bids you walk with him as he shares the treasures of a lifelong journey into the mysteries and meaning of men loving men. *Two Hearts Dancing* will reward you well."

—*WILL ROSCOE*, author of *Queer Spirits: A Gay Men's Myth Book*

"Andrew Ramer is a gifted storyteller and mythmaker. Drawing from imagination, inspiration, his deep understanding of Jewish mysticism, and gay men's spiritual culture, he tells sublime tales that resonate deeply. Andrew and the Maggid Elias are two souls entwined in one body. He/they speak directly to the heart and soul to heal the wounds of millennia of oppression and repression. This book is essential reading for gay men and good medicine for all of humanity."

—*FRANKLIN ABBOTT*, editor of *Boyhood: Growing Up Male*

"You don't read Ramer—you experience him. This is more than a book. It's a primer for transformation, a revelation, a celebration, and an imparting of wisdom that is essential and necessary for us all. Ramer's voice is mythic, indigenous, and of the earth as he shares his vision of what gay people truly are and truly can be—bringers of joy, friendship, creation, love, and healing to those around them."

—*TREBOR HEALEY*, author of *Sweet Son of Pan*

"In poems and stories rich with meaningful metaphors, Andrew Ramer offers the myths of origin for gay men's queer consciousness that orthodox religion has failed to create and which we, therefore, must create for ourselves. Ramer both reveals and exercises the world-creating power of myth. Here are life-affirming, sex-affirming, gay-affirming metaphors to enrich our experience of our lives."

—**TOBY JOHNSON**, author of *Gay Perspective: Things Our [Homo] sexuality Tell Us about the Nature of God and the Universe*

"Andrew Ramer spins the straw of our daily lives into gold. I want to build a campfire and sit around it while he tells stories. 'The passions rise in this, in all new moon nights, slowly, surely, to a full brilliant circle of rich hidden silver.' Indeed."

—**BO YOUNG**, publisher of White Crane Books

Two Hearts Dancing

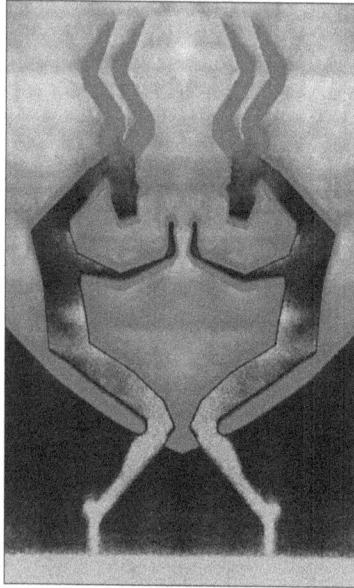

Books by Andrew Ramer

From Wipf and Stock:
  Two Flutes Playing
  Revelations for a New Millennium
  Queering the Text
  Torah Told Different
  Deathless
  Fragments of the Brooklyn Talmud
  The Spiritual Dimensions of Healing Addictions &
  Further Dimensions of Healing Addictions –
      with Donna Cunningham
And:
  Angel Answers
  Ask Your Angels – with Alma Daniel and Timothy Wyllie

Two Hearts Dancing

A Spiritual Journeybook for Gay Men

The Companion Volume to
Two Flutes Playing

Andrew Ramer

with a foreword by Don Shewey

drawings by Raven Wolfdancer

RESOURCE *Publications* • Eugene, Oregon

TWO HEARTS DANCING
A Spiritual Journeybook for Gay Men:
The Companion Volume to Two Flutes Playing

Resource Publications
An Imprint of Wipf and Stock Publishers
199 W. 8th Ave., Suite 3
Eugene, OR 97401

www.wipfandstock.com

PAPERBACK ISBN: 978-1-6667-3060-9
HARDCOVER ISBN: 978-1-6667-2232-1
EBOOK ISBN: 978-1-6667-2233-8

OCTOBER 14, 2021 3:05 PM

for my wise friend Raven Wolfdancer,
for all the men who ever loved men
and all the men who ever will –
in celebration of our sacred role
in the heart of embodied creation.

Table of Contents

Poems for Our Tribe

Foreword

ANDREW RAMER IS A TRICKSTER ELDER. This gay Jewish terrifyingly terraphilic extraterrestrial specializes in writing that blends ancient tribal wisdom with oracular imagination. Yet when you least expect it, he'll come out with some remark that is startlingly silly, dirty, or up-to-date pop-cultural. He succinctly welcomes spring as that moment when tree blossom buds "press out of their tightly covered foreskins."

Many of the beads in this pearl necklace of Ramerian intelligence look like poems, and poems always benefit from being read aloud. But even the pages that don't look like poems invite you to give them body and breath as they work their way into your heart and mind. As a holotropic sequel to *Two Flutes Playing,* the "spiritual journeybook for gay men" that put him on a certain kind of publishing map, *Two Hearts Dancing* comprises a playful picnic basket stuffed with visions, myths, hymns, fables, and prayers, both delicious and intoxicating.

Ramer's sensual shape-shifting storytelling exists as part of a long lineage of literary lap-dancers. You will encounter echoes of pagan/indigenous creation myths going back to *Gilgamesh.* You will find yourself recognizing elements of ecstatic poetry descended from Rumi by way of James Broughton. In his queer retellings of Greek mythology, movies and magazines and designer jeans figure alongside Cole Porter songs, espresso machines, and a homo Minotaur. The eclectic erudition of these pieces conjure (to me, anyway) the slangy, still-harrowing revisit to Grimm's Fairy Tales that Anne Sexton performed with her volume *Transformations.*

"Transformation" is a word that looms large in Ramer's lexicon. One of the biggest blessings of Ramer's writings is the transformative view of gay life and culture that it conveys. Unafraid of unorthodoxy, he freely refers to God while also acknowledging the centrality of touch to gay men's lives. And in his detailed imagining, what qualifies someone to enter the healing realm of sacred touch has less to do with being some kind of sexual acrobat and more to do with a capacity for love.

I find myself thinking about Andrew Ramer's voice. When we refer to a writer's voice, we're usually talking about how their use of words, punctuation, even the arrangement of sentences on the page conveys a world view, a perspective, a personality. Sometimes it's a unified tone, but that's not the case with Andrew. Anyone who has had the pleasure of hearing his speaking voice – at a conference, at a reading, on a podcast, in conversation over dinner or a walk, even just getting his answering machine (yes, he's old school enough to cling to an answering machine rather than electronic voicemail) – retains a sense memory of it. A rich, mellifluous burr, alternately excitable and careful, chatty and performative, his voice continues to operate while he listens, providing an underscore of affirmative wordless interjections, elongated humming, some grunts, some groans, and frequent easy laughter. I say this to invite the reader to make space for the multiplicity and the musicality that pervades these texts as you enjoy the playlist he's conjured for *Two Hearts Dancing*.

Don Shewey
New York City
May 1, 2021

Dancing with Words

MY FIRST GREAT LOVE was ancient Egypt, my second was Greek mythology, and I went off to college in 1969 intending to become an archaeologist. During my junior year abroad I worked in a museum in Jerusalem, cataloging a dig. But the muses had other plans for me, transmuting my love of artifacts from objects to words. In 1976 I was living in Brooklyn, working in a bookstore, when I consciously opened up to the muses, and in 1980 my guides, my gay muses, began to dictate the passages that eventually became *Two Flutes Playing: A Spiritual Journeybook for Gay Men*. Not a handbook for coming out, I think of it (and this book) as guides for "Coming In" – coming in to who we are as a tribe, as a people.

After reading an early version of *Two Flutes Playing*, Raven Wolfdancer (a cofounder of the Gay Spirit Visions Conference) invited me speak at the first gathering, in November 1990. Scared and honored, I shared a podium at GSV with Atlanta poet and therapist Franklin Abbott and Harry Hay – cofounder in 1950 of the Mattachine Society, the second known homosexual rights organizations in the United States, and one of the fathers of the Radical Faerie movement in the 1970s.

At the second GSV conference I read "A Story of Our People," which came to me (all at once) as I was going off to hear Johnny Moses, a Native American storyteller. After listening to that story Raven told me there were more to be written, which I didn't want to hear. But he was right, and more stories about the Walks-Between People began to dance through me, stories grounded in the past and meant to be heard in the present. After seeing a few of Raven's drawings I asked him if he'd do one for each story, but he told me he'd stopped making art. A few months later a letter appeared in the mail – with a new drawing in it! Dancing, playing, a line in a story would inspire another drawing and a line in a drawing would inspire a new story, two different kinds of lines woven together, dancing together.

Raven's murder in 1993 ended our shared journey, and to this day I wonder how our book would have changed and grown if he'd lived. A year after he died I paired the finished stories with his finished drawings, a sketch for another one, added a few more drawings of his so that each story had one, and self-published a 36-page booklet called *Stories of Our People: A Journey-book for Men Who Love Men.* When the first batch sold out I did another printing. Then I put the booklet away – and forgot about it.

GSV changed my life, and for twenty years I had a perfect attendance record. Then I stopped going and didn't return till Covid hit in 2019 and the conference began to meet on Zoom. Speaking at the 2021 Winter Retreat (again with Franklin Abbott) fed me in a soul-deep way. Cut off from the world by Covid, I found myself on a solo writing retreat, feeling more creative than I'd ever felt before. After completing three unfinished novels I decided to organize all my unpublished work – and came upon *Stories of Our People.* I sent a copy to Wipf and Stock (who reissued *Two Flutes Playing*) but they told me it was too short, so I started reading through poems I'd been writing since 1975, most of them forgotten, determined to create a book long enough for them to publish. And they did!

While *Two Flutes Playing* is a collection of the muses' direct words, this book is a collection of words the muses inspired me to write. The first part has all those "Stories of Our People" in it, along with the drawings and sketch Raven did for them. The second part, "Poems for Our Tribe," contains some of my old poems, many of them inspired by my first loves, mythology and archaeology, as you shall soon see. It ends with a story about dying that bookends the first one in this book, which is about being born. (I like to read them both each year at my birthday party.)

This book isn't a sequel to *Two Flutes Playing* but its companion, so you don't have to read it in order to dance into this one. As its companion, I wanted it to have a companion title. At first I called it *Two Hearts Singing,* but that didn't feel active enough. Then *Two Hearts Dancing* rose into consciousness, just as the first story of our people rose up in me all those years ago. As for the dancing hearts – sometimes they're the hearts of a man and his lover, and sometimes they're the hearts of a man and that which my muses and I call Father Earth – dancing their way through the cosmos.

While I hope you find these stories and poems engaging, I'm aware of the ways in which they may seem dated. In the communities I belong to, younger men-who-love-men tend to call themselves queer rather than gay, and the flowering of non-binary and genderqueer identities are only marginally discussed here and in *Two Flutes Playing*. I thought about revising the old pieces, but the archaeologist in me, that collector of artifacts (and my old gay muses) said – "Darling, leave these stories and poems just as you first wrote them." So I did.

These poems and stories are my gifts to you, however you think of yourself and whatever you call yourself. Although they appear on pages of paper, or digitally, they're grounded in the oral tradition – and meant to be read out loud – in bed – to your beloved, beloveds, embodied and otherwise. As with all stories, they're shared with the hope that they'll caress and awaken the stories that live within your heart! The stories and poems of the Walks-Between People. Who come from every other people. And are the hope of a divided world in need of connection and healing on every level – from viruses to the planet himself.

Andrew Ramer
Oakland, California
June 11, 2021

Stories of Our People

When I Was Born

WHEN I WAS BORN, the nurses wrapped me in a yellow blanket. My parents told this story over and over again. How I was such a wonderful baby, such a beautiful baby, that the nurses, the nurses in the hospital, they wrapped me in a yellow blanket.

A yellow blanket. Not a blue one. Or a pink one. No, they wrapped me in a yellow blanket. And every time I heard that story, I got mad.

Blue is for boys. Everyone knows that. And pink is for girls. But what is yellow for? I know that there are planets with more than two choices. But here on Earth, back in 1951, you only got to choose from pink or blue. And frankly, I didn't care which. Boy or girl, girl or boy. Either choice would have been fine with me. But what was my choice?

In a yellow blanket, not blue, or pink, I was sent home from the hospital. And how proud my parents were, of their different, their beautiful, their special little baby.

That story haunted me all through my childhood. Haunted me in the schoolyard, where I sat alone under a tree. Watching the boys play baseball in one corner, while the girls jumped rope in another. It haunted me in the bathtub. It haunted me in my dreams. And it haunted me later, when the hair started growing on my upper lip, in my armpits, beneath my Fruit of the Loom white jockey underpants. Because I looked around me, I looked everywhere, and I didn't see anyone else quite like me. Wrapped up in yellow. Chicken. Scared.

When I was born, the nurses wrapped me in a yellow blanket. Not a blue one or a pink one. And my parents were so proud of that. They told the story over and over. But it took me more than twenty years to own that story. Twenty years to be proud of who I am.

When I was born, six pounds and seven brown ounces, with a head of curly thick black hair, the nurses in the hospital, they wrapped me in a yellow blanket. Not a pink one. Or a blue one. And I'm wrapped in it still. And I ask myself over and over – how did those nurses know, when they wrapped me, newly slipped into this world and still jet-lagged, how did they know, on that new spring night in 1951 – that I would be as different as I am? A walker. Rememberer. And a teller of the stories of our people. That no one else can tell, but one of our people.

4

A Story of Our People

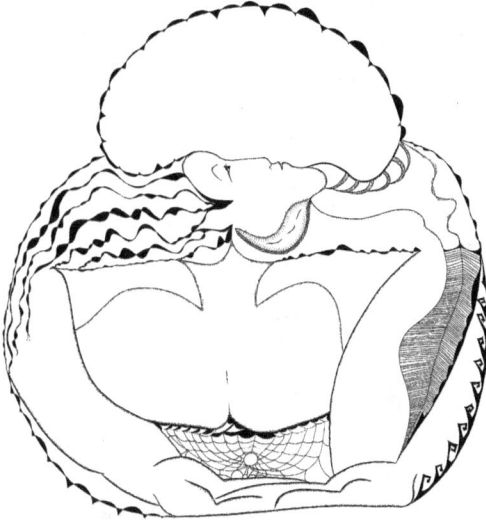

THERE ARE MANY STORIES of our people. Our people have many different names. Sometimes we are called the Man-Woman People, and sometimes we are called the Not Man-Not Woman People. Because of our connection to the air, we are sometimes called the People With Wings, or the Fairy People. And because of our connection to the Earth, we are called the Fruit People and the Faggot People, which means the Bundle of Sticks Tied Together People. We have been called the Fixes the Hair People and the Makes Beautiful Lodges People, and sometimes we are called the Happy People or the Strange People. But of all the names we have called ourselves and been called, my favorite is the Walks-Between People.

After Father Earth had made all the different people, he looked at all of them in their different places, doing their different things and making their different kinds of beauty, and he was very happy. He was happy about everything they were doing. Until he saw that every people was staying in its own place, keeping its own kind of beauty. This made him sad. Very sad. And he wondered who would connect them, who would bring their beauty from one place to another, so that everyone could know all the different kinds of beauty he had made.

This troubled Father Earth. He did not know what to do about it. So he asked Grandmother Sun. She thought about it, and she thought about it, and she thought. She got so tired thinking that she fell asleep. And while she was sleeping, she dreamed. And in her dream, a new kind of people appeared, the Walks-Between People – the People who walk between women and men, who walk between night and day, who walk between the sky and the earth, who walk between the living and the dead, connecting them, carrying their beauty from place to place.

When Grandmother Sun awoke, the Walks-Between People were being born among all the different peoples. This made her very happy. For whenever we appear among them, we connect them. And wherever we appear among them – we find each other and we carry their beauty back and forth and back and forth. Now, by our love, all the different people can see all the beauty that there is. And this makes Father Earth happy. This makes him very happy. For we are a Connecting People. And we are also a Mysterious People. No one knows where we come from, or where we will appear. And they never will. Yes, we are a Mysterious People, and whenever they see us, we remind all the other people of the Great Mystery. Which is a good thing. A very good thing.

Two Men Walking

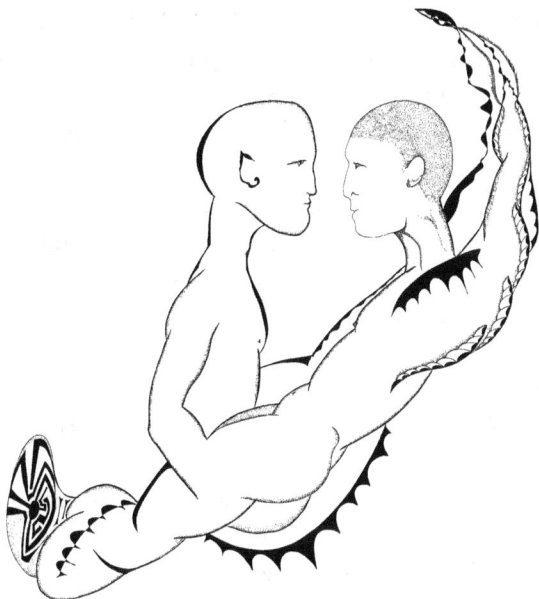

BEFORE THERE WERE EVER two men walking together on the broad and beautiful body of Father Earth, no one walked here. This was so long ago that Sky didn't know if it was Mother or Father yet. And Earth didn't know if it was Father or Mother. This was in the time when all beginnings and all endings were still connected, like a wolf cub biting its own tail.

All the people were here then, and all the people were finding out what it meant to be alive. They were hearing their own songs, and they were dancing to them. But no one had begun to walk yet. And then, Mother Sky dreamed the Walks-Between People, the flower of her dreaming. She dreamed them, and they started to be born. Two were born then, two boys on either side of the world. And they grew tall and strong, in the shelter of their families. But their heads were always turning, eyes and ears hungry, hungry for something that they could not find around them.

One of them was as tall as an oak. He was strong as a bear. He was as far-seeing as a hawk, and he moved across the land with the same grace as a dolphin. His skin was green as the forests, and his eyes were golden as the sun.

Far away, on the other side of the world, lived another Walks-Between man. He was as proud as a lion, as beautiful as a willow. He was as gentle as a deer, and he moved across the land with the wisdom of an owl. His skin was indigo, and his eyes were as silver as the moon.

With the power of an eagle when it cuts across the sky, the power of a pine tree when it splits a granite outcropping, sinks roots in, and flourishes – with that very same power, these two men heard each other's song. They heard each other's song and began to search for each other. They said good-bye to their families and began to walk. By day they walked, singing and coming closer to each other. By night they dreamed, they dreamed each other's song. By day their feet touched every part of the world. By night they dreamed all the pleasures they would find when they sang in their bodies together.

Fiercely they walked. They walked for so long that they made days and weeks and seasons and years beneath their feet. They met on top of Turquoise Mountain. Their eyes met, their hearts met, their arms and their lips and their bodies met. The song they sang together made beauty happen. Earth heard it, and was filled with beauty. Sky heard it too, and was filled with beauty too. "This is a good people," they said, taking pleasure in the two men's pleasure. And from out of that pleasure, all over the world, other Walks-Between People started to be born.

And whenever two men meet to sing their body songs, the First Two Men fill them and sing with them again, the blue and the green man. Yes, they sing with them, they walk with them, they fill them. And because we come from every other people, we carry pleasure in our bodies for all of them.

The Guardians of the Trees

THE WORLD WAS STILL new. People were still new. And one day Father Earth went walking amongst them. He saw how they moved in the beautiful world he had made. It was summer, a beautiful summer, warm and clear and sweet smelling of grasses and flowers and trees. And Father Earth called all the people to him, to gather together in one place. And the people heard his call, and they met him in a hidden valley, in a grove, beside a mountain stream.

"In this world," he said, "each of you carries a task." He appointed the men and women who love each other to stand at the doorway of life and to be the guardians of the children. He gave the women who love women the task of being the guardians of the animals. To the Blind tribe he gave stewardship of the minerals of the earth. To the Deaf tribe he gave stewardship of the waters. And he made the men who love men the guardians of the trees. And he counseled all the people to hold fast to their stewardships, for the good of his earth, and for the good of all who live here. That was a long time ago, in the first world, when everything was still new.

And hasn't it always been that way, that men who love men have loved trees? Even before we knew we were lovers of men, didn't we love the trees, and turn to their strong dark leafy arms for comfort, in world after world after world? And here in the fourth world, didn't we once meet in sacred groves, to dance, to sing, to love? And when the people of this world forgot the powers of all the tribes, didn't we still turn to the trees, to meet there in secrecy, to gather there, to find each other there?

When Pieter was small, he used to climb up in the branches of an elm tree. And oh, the dreaming he did there. Adam's favorite tree was tall. He lay on the earth, curled between two thick winding roots. Omar loved the date palms, his belly pressed flat, his arms wrapped tight when he climbed them. Wing ran through the bamboo, feeling the press of their leaves on his skin. Kwame climbed high, so high through thick leaves that he could look out over the village, and see the distant mountains. Carlos slept in a hammock, hanging from the branches of a tree his great-grandfather had planted, singing himself to sleep night after night. And when they were older, in the night, when a single candle burned, when moonlight only lit their room, when everything was still, in that magic place after love-making, each of them told their lovers about the trees they had loved in boyhood. Describing the bark, the leaves, the feel. As if they were talking about a lover. Yes, remembering their first lover. For we are the guardians of the trees. This flows in our blood. We cannot escape it, however much we may forget it.

The trees call out to us. In the wind, they call us. In storm. In night. In spring, when the first buds press out of their tightly covered foreskins, red or yellow or pale new green. In summer, rich of vibrant green. In winter, bare. The trees call out to us. And we, in our deepest hearts, we too call out to them. So like them in our nature, female and male together. Tall, supple, strong, sweet lifeblood surging upward.

The Forest Birthing

IN THEIR TENDER DANCE of love, he was like Father Earth and she was like Mother Sky. And in the moment when new life began to hum within her body, she knew it. She lay awake all night in their lodge, laughing to herself with pleasure. In the morning, when Grandmother Sun came up over the mountains, she turned to her mate and said to him, "There is a life within my body." And he felt it too. And they were happy.

As that life grew, the two of them sang to it, laughed with it, told it stories. And after several moons had passed, the life within this mother's body began to turn and move. She reached down to it and felt the presence of one about to arrive. And she knew by the way that the child within her danced, and by the songs he sang in her body, that he was coming to her from the Walks-Between People. And she told her mate, who put his hand on her belly and felt the stirring. And he knew also that this child would be a son. And he knew also that this son would be a Walks-Between man. And they were happy.

In the morning of a beautiful spring day, when the crocuses were in bloom, the mother withdrew to the birthing lodge at the edge of the village – with her mate. Rocking and singing, squatting in his arms, she gave birth to a son. And they called him Shining Flower, for the crocuses in the meadow were as golden as he was, shining in their arms. And they were happy.

As the boy grew, his parents and his family and his tribe saw him and loved him and told him all the stories of their people. His father told him the men's stories. And his mother told him the women's stories. And whenever anyone from the Walks-Between camp came to visit, they would take their son to him, to be held and rocked, so that he could hear those stories too. And he was happy.

In a lodge in the center of the village, painted with sun, moon and stars, Shining Flower grew strong and tall. And in the season when the hair of his body began to grow, his father and mother packed him a three-day journey's worth of food. And his mother gave him the shawl she had embroidered for him. And his father gave him the flute that he had carved for him and painted. And they blessed him as they stood beside him on the hill at the edge of their village. And they pointed to the forest path that led to the Walks-Between camp.

Shining Flower cried as he stood between his mother and his father. His tears were tears of sorrow and of joy. For he knew that it was time to leave his parents. And he knew that it was time to find his people. He knew that he would return to the village, when he had learned all the stories of his people, the songs and the dances. And he knew in his body that it was time to go. So when his breath was full, in the middle of his body, he thanked his parents, swung his pack over his shoulders – and walking with a strong proud step, he began the journey home.

The People Who Worshipped Everything

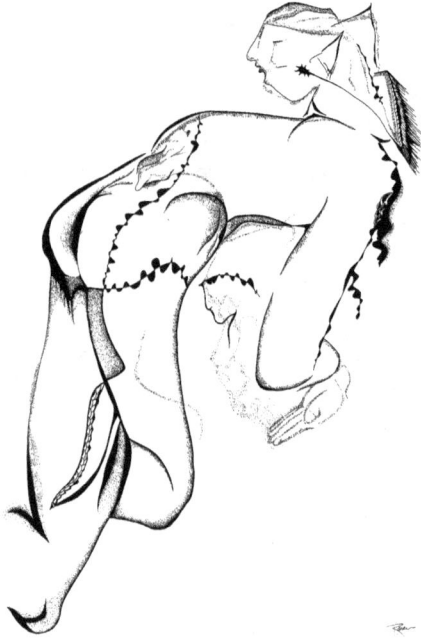

ONCE, OUR PEOPLE WORSHIPPED trees. For this, other people killed us, when they came to our sacred camps. Our people had always worshipped trees, for their voices carry the whisper of the Great Mystery.

Once, our people worshipped the rocks, and especially the mountains on the horizon. We woke to those mountains and prayed to them. For us they were a ladder to the stars. But other people came on horses, and they saw the way that our people worshipped the mountains. And they said that we were blind to the real God in the sky. And they killed us.

Once, our people worshipped animals. We worshipped the deer and the eagle and the turtle and the bear especially. Each in their own way reminded us of our Father, the Earth. When we saw them, when we saw them moving through the world, we saw another part of the spirit of our Father made flesh, and we worshipped that. But other people came, they came with their guns and they said that we were a childish people, a people who were wrong. They could not understand why we worshipped the animals. And because of that, they killed us.

Once, our people worshipped everything, for we are the ones who walk between night and day, who walk between women and men, who walk between the living and the dead, who walk between earth and sky. We worshipped all the worlds and places we walked through. But other people came along with a god they said was Love, and they saw the way that we loved, and they called us evil. And because they saw us as evil, they killed us in our lodges made of trees or skins, and in our villages made of stone. They killed us. They killed us again and again. But we are back now. We are back in the minds of their children. We are back in the hearts of their grandchildren. We are back, we are back in the bodies of their great-grandchildren.

Yes, we are back. We are back to worship the trees again, the air, the water, the birds, the sky, the land. We are back to love each other again. Tell me, is this evil? To worship everything that is, because everything that is, is truly a part of the One who made it.

The Lodge of Our People

IN THE MOON OF the big sun, Shining Flower came to the lodge of our clan, the Walks-Between People. He sat in the lodge with the men of our clan and the elders of our clan. He smoked with them the pipe that was made by our clan ancestor, Comes From Turquoise Mountain. He learned from them the ancient ways of our people. He learned our songs and our ceremonies.

When the moon had died and been born again three times, the elders took the young man into the mountains. They took away his boy clothing, they smudged him and bathed him and sat with him in the sweat lodge. Then they gave him the clothes of a man of our people. And they gave him a man's name, Red Oak so that he could live in the world in the Walks-Between way.

Now there was a man of our people named Four Hawks, who was drawn to Red Oak. He was drawn to him as the men of our people are drawn to each other. And Four Hawks reached out to Red Oak in the way that the men of our people first reach out to other men. He reached out to Red Oak with his eyes.

Red Oak let Four Hawks touch him with his eyes. And he touched him back. Then Four Hawks touched Red Oak with the hands of his body, and Red Oak touched him back. Yes, they touched each other in the ways of our people.

Because of the way that Red Oak touched Four Hawks, Four Hawks felt new life in his body. He grew heavy and swollen till he could not move. The elders and the ancestors had to come and feed him. Red Oak sat with him all this time, waiting. And when the moon had made nine journeys into death and life again, Four Hawks gave birth to a story. He gave birth to the story that Red Oak had made him pregnant with. This is his story.

> In the last world there were two men who shared a lodge. Their lodge was painted with the sign of the flute players. This was in the days when Grandmother Sun had gotten so old that it was time for her to die again. She was

curled up in her bed so small beneath her blankets that the people could not tell if it was night or day, or day or night.

The elders gathered all the people together. They said that it was time to go to a new world. But there was so little light that it was hard to find this new world.

In the darkness no one saw how with the last little bit of Grandmother's fire, the men who shared a lodge had taken their flutes and climbed to the top of the mountains.

When they got to the top of the mountains, they took out their flutes and they played them. Then all of the people knew where to climb, and they followed the music up the mountain to the new world that we live in today. And it was here that Grandmother Sun was born again.

Because these two men who shared a lodge had played their flutes that way, in our new world – we are consciousness scouts for all the people, and it is still the men of our tribe who lead the other people to new places.

Desire's First Breath

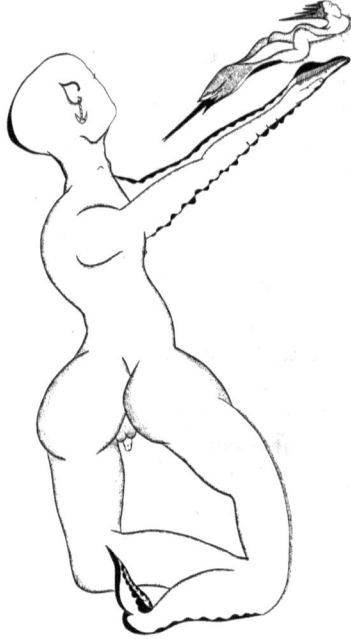

TOGETHER, WE RISE UP from dreaming. Out of time. Up from the silence, up into the light of day. For a single moment, your smile is before me. And then you vanish, you vanish into morning. I am alone again. But in my heart, you are still with me. Face, forgotten. Name, forgotten. Feeling of you, remembered.

Half-remembered. My heart longs for you. I see you dancing round a fire. And my heart, my heart is filled with longing. There is no room in my ribcage for it. Heart pushes up against the walls of my chest, ready to explode like a stone in a fire pit. And you dance around the fire. It is night. There is music. There is a circle of dancers, all of them young men. All of them turning. But it is you. Your body. Your foot as it touches the earth, that beats the drum of my heart again and again. Cock pushing up against the sheets for you. Half-remembered. And then fading. Only the night, the circle, the feeling of you.

The room is flooded with light. The windows are open. Birds call from the tree next to the house, crabapple, covered with tiny white blossoms. And the roof of the house next door is covered with lilacs. Heavy, swollen, I wake to their lavender sweetness. You fade, and lilac fills the empty spaces. The two, the same. Filling me. Intoxicating.

All through the day, you are with me. You, half-remembered. The feel of you, beside me. Presence, invisible. I turn as I walk, expecting to see you at every corner. Inspecting every face I see, boy after boy, man after man, looking.

Sometimes, in the silence, I can hear the music. Sometimes, for a moment, eyes look back at me as you would. And the smell of lilac is heavy as I slide between the sheets. And the darkness wraps itself around me, when I turn the light off next to my bed. And the dream of you fills my body again, surging, calling out for touch. Hard, calling out for touch. My touch, which pretends to be you. The dream of you calling out to me again. Slipping into it. As hand rocks me back to you, down to you, out to you again.

The Power of the Hand Tribe

WE ARE CALLED BY many names in this world. Some are beautiful and some are cruel. Some are beautiful and some are false. We are called by many names in this world. And we call ourselves by many different names. One of the names we call ourselves is the Hand Tribe.

We call ourselves that because we carry things. Because we carry beauty from place to place, because we are artists, always have been and always will be, the makers of beautiful things. But we call ourselves that especially because we are the bearers of touch for all the people, the bearers of heart-fire, the bearers of healing. We are the ones who have risked damnation, prisons, excommunication, institutionalization, and even death, simply because we needed to touch each other. No other people could do this, risk death as we do, simply to lay hands upon each other's flesh. To some of us this has been a curse, this desire. But in our sacred groves, we know this is our power, to carry the love of touch to a world that has so come to fear it.

Once, everyone knew that the world itself is holy, the holy body of our Father. Once, everyone knew that all of life upon our Father's body is holy. Once, everyone knew that we ourselves are holy, that we choose our bodies to express our holiness in the world. And we use our bodies to express our holiness with each other, when we dance the dance of love.

But people have forgotten this. Our bodies are wounded, our air and water are poisoned, our earth is deeply scarred. And who can tell the peoples of the world that our bodies are holy? Only we can, the Hand Tribe, the people who remember how to touch in a sacred way. And who will tell the peoples of the world that the world itself is holy? We will. The Hand Tribe. The people who make beautiful things that reveal the wonders of our Father Earth.

Touch yourself – and know that you are holy. When you touch someone else – know that they are holy too. Raise your hands up to the sky and know that it is holy. Place your hands upon the Earth and know that it is holy too. You are a holy one. All people are holy. The standing people, crawling people, flying people, swimming people, the four leggeds, the cloud people, the stone people, the air people. All people are holy. And we of the Hand Tribe, we are the ones who carry the memory of this knowing to all the people.

He Who Comes Walking

IN THE DAY, HE comes walking. I can hear him coming. I can hear him coming from years away. His footsteps are silent. And yet I hear him coming, hear him walking, walking from far away.

In the night, he comes walking. I can hear him in my dreams. I can hear him coming closer, coming softly. I can feel him walking toward me in my dreams. He climbs a mountain. Like a ram he scales its peaks. Like a cougar he moves though its forests. Like an eagle his eyes are searching.

I hear him all the time. I hear him walking toward me. His breath is on my cheek. Long before I ever felt the sweet breath of another man beside me, I dreamt of his breath on my cheek, while I lay sleeping.

When I touched you, Joseph, I was looking for his skin. When I kissed you, Roberto, I was remembering his lips. Richard, Stuart, David, Edward, Neil. In the eyes, the arms, the cock, legs, belly, ass of every man I ever touched, I was touching him, I was remembering him, I was searching for the wandering pieces of him, spread out across the world.

He was looking for me. He dived to the bottom of the sea. Like a fish, like a dolphin, like a whale, he searched but he did not see me, could not hear me, did not find me, telling you this tale.

I take the world. I make of it words. I tell the stories of our people. Like an elder of our people, I sit in the dark of night and tell our stories. Singing and chanting, crying and laughing, I tell all the stories that ever were and ever will be. From the beginning I tell them, from the beginning of time. I tell of the first men, the green man and the blue man. I tell all the stories of all the men who ever loved another man. I tell them in words, I paint them in words of ochre and umber and black.

Just as I am finishing the last story, and washing in the stream of mind my paint-colored hand – He Who Comes Walking, turns the corner of the canyon. It is you, and you come from the north end of the canyon. Your feet are in the water, your head is in the clouds, shining, and ringed with bright stars. You come toward me, strong and gentle. I see you as you turn the last bend in the canyon. You see me, and call out my name. I am Waits By The River. And I call to you your own true name. And slowly, you walk toward me, as I dreamed you would when I was still a boy. In the canyon, in the water. In the stories that I told. You come close and then closer. You, no longer walking. I, no longer waiting. We two men together now, body to body. In the air, in the water, on the earth. On fire.

How We Will Be
In the Next World

ONCE ALL THE LIGHT was inside of us. All the light we needed. In those days, no one had shadows because we were all radiant, even in the darkest nights. That was in the last world. But in this world, we have been afraid. In this world, we have hidden our light. In this world, there is more light outside us than within. In this world, us have shadows.

In the last world, we were a funny people. We used our joy to make laughter for all the people. But in this world we have forgotten our laughter. Listen to us in the places where we gather. Is anyone laughing there? Laughing the joy laugh? No. The only laugh left to us has been the cutting laugh, the hurting laugh, the looking down upon everyone else laugh. The laugh that comes from our own wounds. This laugh is our shadow.

Once we were the people who made beauty and carried it from place to place. That was in the last world. But in this world our eyes are veiled over, and we can no longer distinguish two shades of a color where others see but one. And look at us in the darkened places where we gather. Are they beautiful places? No. And while we make beauty for others, the only beauty we make for ourselves we hide, or we hide in. This hiding is our shadow.

Once we were a loving and compassionate people. That was in the last world. But in this world we have become bitter. We come to judge each other and ourselves, to use each other body and spirit, to fear the love we carry in our hearts. When we gather, how often are our eyes clouded over, or glaring? How often are we looking down upon each other. This comes from how small we feel inside. This lack of loving is our shadow.

But now – our elders are gathering again. They are climbing out from dark and hidden places. They are finding the flicker of light they still carry within. They are feeling it, fanning it, and sharing it with others.

Come, let us light our inner fires. Let us sit as once we sat before, illuminated by our laughter, our beauty and our love. Together, we are making a new world. Together we are finding our light again. For ourselves, and for those of our tribe who will follow us, shining.

When We Are Very Old

YOU SLEEP IN MY arms. Your back pressed to my belly. I can feel the tremor in your body, the dance of your dreaming. Then you are still, your breath coming soft and even. I bend my lips to the side of your neck. In the stillness of our bed, as the first light of morning whispers its song. You wake, and press your body close to me. The heat of your body warms me as no layering of blankets ever can. Like the sun, the fire of my body wakens. I turn your face to meet me. Wet, my tongue seeks out the tongue of you, speaking the language of two bodies that fifty years of talking have turned into one.

I roll on top of you, my beloved. There where you wait, I find you. Soft belly pressed to soft belly, soft breast pressed down to soft breast. And we are eye to eye now, my beloved. Back and forth between our eyes, dancing bridges are built of ropes flung over the rock walls of a canyon. Across this rope bridge, deer walk, bear walk, birds fly, squirrels scamper, all of life goes back and forth and back and forth between us.

Your hands on my back pull me down to you. Eye to eye, my tongue explores your face. In the wrinkles round your eyes there are rivers. Rivers flowing thick with life. Fish swim in these rivers, frogs, turtles, fresh water dolphins. I am lost in these rivers, my beloved. I am lost in the cry of whales screaming up from the sea of your breath.

I take your face in my hands. Run my fingers through your hair. Each silver hair is a story. I listen to them all. What richness of years are in your stories. Time. Wisdom. Love. Our bodies rock. Slowly. I press into your stories. Tree-root of my body pressed to tree-root of your body. Skin opening to skin.

We are so old, my beloved. Time itself stops in our embracing. Days, nights, morning, all of them are still in our bodies. Even the earth now is still. Stopped. Only the sigh of you, breath of you, singing into my body-sighs. And birds fly out of your mouth, clouds, stars, lightning. Like a man who has danced all night, I stagger into your eyes. Fall all the way down into your body. We are one. And oneness only is happening in this bed of dreaming. Holy oneness. On fire. Racing. Liquid fire. Screaming the bliss of creation. Darkness. Then your body explodes into opal liquid light. Together, we explode. And from that moment of darkness, the mother of all suns is born again from our bodies. Floating on a sea of liquid pearls. Brilliant. Giving birth to whole new worlds. Thundering. Hearts thundering. You and I again, heart to heart. Together. Containing everything.

Midwives for the Dying

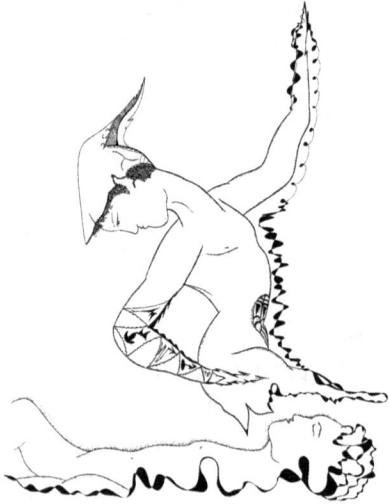

"WHO WILL STAND AT the closing door?" Father Earth asked all the people. "Who will guide the dying into the next world?" Because we walk from place to place. Between women and men. Between night and day. Between earth and sky. Between every nation. Because of that, we stand by the starry door. Always have. Always will. To hold someone's hand. To whisper in their ear, "All is well. You are not alone. I can see your friends on the other side, gathered already to meet you."

Nahr, in his cave, in the depths of cold, stood by that door and guided others through it. Tapak in his jungle, Uhuli in his forest, Walid in his desert, Erik on the top of his high mountain. And Toshi on the island he calls home. Roberto in the heart of a noise-filled city. And Pavel and Teddy and Manolo and Jean-Claude. By cots, on floors, leaning over hospital beds. Since the beginning of time, we have midwifed the dying. We have midwifed the dying, and we always will.

You hold me in your arms, rocking me, singing. You tell me stories. Recite to me poems. You wipe my forehead. You slip little diamond chips of ice between my sky blue lips. You tuck my big bright yellow blanket close around me. Lay your head on the pillow beside me. And you whisper. Tell me stories. You tell me all the stories of our people. And all the stories of the next world. Eagles guard the windows. Deer stand by the door. A golden bear lies dreaming underneath my bed. While back and forth, back and forth you go. Back and forth between the worlds, forth and back you walk. Back and forth with words for me. Dreams for me. Visions. Rocking me. Holding me in your strong and tender arms.

The room is filled with light now. Everything is illuminated. Bed, chairs, walls, floor. Me, You. The air itself. All glowing. Light pouring in through a door that only you and I can see. Grandmother Sun's bright golden light pouring in. As ancestors gather to meet me, gather to meet me on the far side of that door. As you hold my hand. As you lean to kiss my forehead. As everything grows silent. As everything bursts into song. The song of the ancestors. The song of all worlds. And I turn to you one last time, turn to kiss you. Then, I walk through the door to Great Mystery. I walk through that door. No, I fly.

The Seed Bearer

How it was and will be – is how it is, always. That the one who listens, the one who walks, the one who remembers, the one who becomes, he is the one who carries the seed for all of us.

There is a bird, a bird both male and female, a bird both dead and alive, a bird both matter and spirit, both angel and human – and that bird is the one who carries the seed for all of us.

The man is the bird. The man is flying. He is flying from world to world. No. He is not flying. There is nowhere for him to fly to. For he fills all space. He is space.

The man who is winged, who flies and does not fly, who carries the seed for all of our people, he sits in council, sits in silence, sits with an ear turned to each world. And the dead, speak. And the living, speak. And the dead, listen. And the living, listen.

The elders sit in council. They sit in council never-ending. And the lodge they sit in, isn't it under the clear blue vault of heaven? Isn't it under the starry black vault of heaven? And isn't it one lodge, always? Both day and night, and night and day, always?

The words, the silence. The silence, the visions. In this lodge, how it was and how it will be, is always being born. Poised, perfect, each moment whole, like a pearl. Each moment, one and the same. And the pearl of all time is the seed in the heart of the man of our people. It is all seeds. All ways.

And who are you, I ask? Aren't you the man? Aren't you the elder? Aren't you the shining, the seed bearing flower? Aren't you the one whose wings spread out and touch the walls of our lodge that is earth and heaven? Yes, I know you. I know you are that man. God. Dreamer. Spirit. Angel. Female and male. Living and dead. Yes. You are the one. You are the seed bearer. You are the whole. You are wrapped in a shawl of gold that is everything. Everything. Always.

Responsory for Walks-Between Gatherings

ONCE WE WERE A great and glorious people.
>With what we all embodied, we would heal the world.

We were shamans and elders and priests and seers.
>With what we all embodied, we would heal the world.

We were artists and dancers and poets and teachers.
>With what we all embodied, we would heal the world.

Then our temples and holy places were destroyed.
>With what we have had to learn, we could heal the world.

Our love was reviled, called an abomination.
>With what we have had to learn, we could heal the world.

We were hunted and tortured for hundreds and hundreds of years.
>With what we have had to learn, we could heal the world.

Like bundles of wood, we were burned at the stake.
>With what we have had to learn, we could heal the world.

The hateful names we were called still shout in our minds.
>With what we have had to learn, we could heal the world.

In silence we lived, afraid to tell our stories.
>With what we have had to learn, we could heal the world.

We met in dark places, if we met at all, faceless, ashamed.
>With what we have had to learn, we could heal the world.

Defying death, we found each other.
>With what we have had to learn, we will heal the world.

Our lives were not whole, and yet we lived them.
>With what we have had to learn, we will heal the world.

We could not touch in the streets, and in many places we still can't.
>With what we have had to learn, we will heal the world.

So many of us died, in the blood of our wounds.
>With what we have had to learn, we will heal the world.

But in the midst of our suffering, we are finding each other.

With what we have had to learn, we will heal the world.
We are remembering our songs, we are showing our faces,
    With what we have had to learn, we will heal the world.

We are lovers and dreamers, we are healers and warriors.
    With what we have had to learn,
    We are owning our power,
    We are owning our beauty,
    We are owning our wisdom,
    We are owning our visions,
    We are owning our heart-fire,
    We are growing together,
    We are dancing and singing,
    In light, love, and purpose,
    We are all stepping forward,
    For the Earth and all people,
    And with all that we have to share –
    We are healing this world.

Poems for Our Tribe

Invocation

I want to do one thing only
put together this and that
the way my mother whipped together
flour and milk
to make her crepe batter
bubbling in the hot buttery pan
when she poured it in

I want to do two things at the same time
just like my father did
when he strapped a harmonica to his jaw
and played it
as his nimble fingers strummed
his shiny steel-stringed guitar

I want to mix together
sing together
the way that I love men
with the way that I love
the world

I want to whip
stir
mix
play
chant and sing
the two together
till both are edible
both are holy
eaten together
sung together

in one place
wholly
here
with words

The Temple of Father Earth
and Mother Sky

KUNIATA WENT DOWN, DOWN into the rushes and the wailing. Down into the need. Down by the flowing stream. Down into the valley of his people. In the old days. In the long days of the year. It was then that Kuniata went down. Down to listen to the crying of his people. By the rushes. In the heat. In the long days of summer. In the far and away years. In the years long before you were born. In those years, in that time, it was then that Kuniata went down. Kuniata, the Elder-Priest of his people.

To the east, there were the Nokappi. To the west the Rahunda lived. In the south, in the south, were still and always mountains. And in the north, to the north, was the great inland sea, then and always. But the world was changing. Humankind was changing. With anger first. Then blood. Carried on the voices of the people. Voices of bleeding and despair. For the Nokappi and the Ohuay who lived in the valleys to the east, who lived in the valleys to the east of the Seefe, the Seefe who were Kuniata's people. Yes, the Ohuay were setting out against the Seefe. Seefe farmers and Seefe hunters. They were setting out with long bows and sharp spears. Great Lady Tand, the leader of the Seefe, the gentle Seefe, the long-lived Seefe in their grass and reed huts, she and her people were dying at the hands of the Ohuay raiders. And that was why Kuniata went down, hearing their cries, went down with his Feather Men and their drums and their chants. He the Elder of the Walks-Between People. He went down. Down from the open hills that were the home of his good people.

It was then, and it was there, it was in Yahl-wah-tay, the Place where Animals Cross the Water, it was there and it was then that the vision came to Kuniata. Of a temple, a great temple, a temple to preserve not the old ways but the deep ways, the ways that are deep in human hearts. Yes, it came to Kuniata to build a temple, and he marked out the lines of it in the dirt, just as they were shown to him. Yes, he marked those lines that became walls and lodgings and healing rooms, lines his followers built upon to create the outer court and the inner shrine of the temple of his vision, his vision of Nas-mahay Tal-wah-hahn – the Temple of Father Earth and Mother Sky. Because the world was changing. And never had there been temples before. No. Our people had always prayed and sang and danced out in the open, out beneath the bright or starlit body of holy Mother Sky. And they sang and danced in illuminated caves, all the way back in time. Caves deep in the hard hard body of our holy Father Earth. But he, Kuniata, and those like us, who were Walks-Between priests for all the people, they knew the world was changing, that it was time for us to worship in new ways. And thus the first temple on this world was born, in the north of what we now call Africa, by the great inland sea.

And Kuniata the Wise served there, and passed on the priesthood to his beloved Relag. And Relag too passed on the priestly elderhood. And this is the lineage of the twenty-six elder-priests in the Temple of Father Earth and Mother Sky, in the days and years before the patriarchal priests took over the temple and put an end to the work that we were doing, we who were Walks-Between elders for all the people. Yes, this is the lineage of our Elder-Priests at Yahl-wah-tay:

Kuniata
Relag
Arandakah
Nu-hammad
Arrasu
Sandath
Mahandaq
Kur
Ni-andah
Ratmahil
Rikur
Nandak
Rith-mahay
Turka-hayah

Mardahl
Rihan
Talway
Hutan-kay
Nahandah
Ramintak
Drur
Indrur
Lathmah-handah
Indik
Tal-mas
Rin-tas . . .

Poor Rintas our final priest, whose successor would have been Nasmad-hayah, both of them killed by the armed priests of the new chief god of the people of the valley of Yahl-wah-tay, in the days when the chieftains of Egypt were unifying the villages of the Nile river valley and the Nile delta into two united kingdoms for the first time. When people still remembered some things but were forgetting others. That now we can remember, from the legacy of our ancient Elder-Priests. Can remember, we and all the people. Can remember, as we return to Father Earth and Mother Sky. As we return to the ways of peace. As we return to loving the holy world that is our sacred home. We of the Walks-Between Tribe, for all the people. We who are born to be wise and holy.

Listening Brothers

Listening brothers
we
turning the world
back and forth between us
and giving it to the people

Blood brothers
we
turning to source
of ancient night chant
and giving our songs
to the people

Body brothers
we
bound as the wish bone
in sky-bird's azure breast
blessed
in our giving out blessings

Listening brothers
we
thunder
on horse
men
thundering

Brooklyn Bridge Poem

I have a part in this
span between
split rock and
rock island.
Mountains, artificial
rear themselves
into
the haze of day
powder blue
pierced
by clouds, gulls, jets.

Once
this arching
would have defined the horizon.
Now, swallowed by it
with blue Manhattan Bridge
echoing beside it.
Caught in this disjointed
fucking of boroughs.
Swathed in nets
scaffolds and repair cables
it stands
pylonic entryway
to future ruin.
Pummeled by the constant noise of
traffic.

I sit alone
outside its shadow
on a bench
in the squeak of pier,
a kind of bridge myself.
Sloughed like the river
slushing through it
connecting
rock and rock,
water and
water.

I watch you
kneeling
at the edge of a beam
with nothing
not net or rigging between you
and the brittle gray surface of water.
Squatting, with complete disregard
for potential disaster
sawing
muscles bunched and flexing
as you talk to a fellow worker
astride and as close in my eye
to your death
as this bridge
beneath
your
beefy
ass.

Four Categories of Men

He isn't a god
and
he cannot dance.

He isn't a god
but he dances.

He is a god
but
he cannot dance.

He is a god
and oh
the way he dances!

I Saw a Man

I saw a man so beautiful
that planets ceased to move
and heart
on meeting his clear gaze
quick died for half a beat

And only
when the train doors closed
and roared and pulled away
when he was sealed
in memory
did I start
walking home

Father Earth Triptych

I

Stream, Papa
your stomach gurgles like mine
must have inherited that from you.
Smell of you, old man
pungent, witch hazel
wet mossy damp earth
walking through your fragrant armpit.
Your back is hairy, Dad
never noticed before
and now that I mention it
I like you raw like this
down here alone
me, my brothers, and big old you
in need of a haircut
I hope you don't get.

II

If I was a cock with feet
and you were
hand mouth asshole
my life would be
fucking my way into you
over and over
till I die.
Oh, sometimes falling asleep
after I come to a new place
and sometimes going soft in you
cause I'm turned on by something else
book TV good meal
long telephone conversation

those lesser gods that
you (unlike some others)
are never jealous of
but push me toward
with wild abandon

III

If Whitman
were here with us
Sophocles
Jesus
Michelangelo
Rumi
Basho
men who did or
might have
would they feel
not just us
but you
Earth god
Pan
penicillin
for wounded hearts
and gay souls
first man
horny Earth
slipping your soft
wet body into me
with every breath

Invocation/Out-Vocation

It isn't the circle we cast
(inaccurate – an oval would be so much truer).

It isn't the four directions we invoke
(or is it seven – up down center?)

It isn't the
outfit
garments
cloaks
shoes
makeup
styles
colors
or being naked.

It isn't
the time
season
reason
cause
occasion.

What we gay men
bring to our rituals
that no one else can
is what I once heard our elder
Harry Hay
(or was it his partner
John Burnside?)
call
"the silly sacred."

Incantation

Color of wind and weight of fire
Turn in the heart of this ancient desire

Whisper of earth
Pure light of sea
Open our hands
And draw us closer.

New Dreams

Where alchemy divides the world in two
And magic makes of love's male/female art
We know the multiplicity of form
That separates each single heart from heart.

In fabled place that still lives on in dream
Beyond the world of word that has denounced
A silent place that mirrors can't reveal
As photographs cannot remember voice.

For in our age a newer magic is born
To vapors, mountains, parents, children, dreams
That circles not as it stoops to transform
But turns elliptic in post-Copernican scheme.

For seldom pictures of this world do show
The fullness of the human heart's true growth.

In Bed Without You

If I turn the corner
you are in the room.
Eyes the color of a hand
on the side of my face.

You are the one I have been waiting for
since 1918
or since that morning in 1411
when you picked up your saddle
and left.

A gypsy fortune teller at a flea market
said to me Child,
your desires are strange –
and they will find you.

I have my pajamas on now.
They are white
the buttons all popped away
one by one as I slept.
Were they your hands
Philippe
working your hunger toward my flesh?

There was a time
when I believed you would come.
You were a prayer
mantra.
You were the meal I was forever
waking to the smell of,
kitchen smoky and hot.
You were the cloud that turns
into another cloud.

You were the surprise in every box.

If I touch myself
it isn't the same thing.
I may hold my face
but I cannot look back.

How many people
go to bed without you, Walid?
How many people become the bed
long before the sun of your kisses
rises over their wide hungry mouth?

I bunch up the cover.
What do you do?
I grab where you might be
in an early hours film.

The bed is stained.
I am broken.
Where the laugh used to be
Noburu
you haven't even sent a postcard.

Night Magic

How often have I stood beside night sea
and watched incoming waves break
as do mountains
which turn their furious wrath upon the beach
where dissipated, humbled, make pale fountains?

How many nights at altar by the sea
hands outstretched above a blue-flamed fire
have I invoked the goddess of the lee
while you stood there beside me
playing lyre?

And then we hand in hand neared that dark face
grown still as kneeling beasts upon the shore
bejeweled host of dragons sleeping now
sprawled flat their outstretched flanks a perfect mirror
where in the darkness that reflects moon's face
is seen the luminous silver of love's grace

Spun

Spun indigo limbs in the darkness
trace me
across the moonless plain
from thigh to nipples.

The soft tip of your up
and downward flowing finger
tingles me more
than the infinite night's
white pin pricks.

Your hard is soft
as the new moon night
that arches us over
into a slow
blue black bathed kiss.

There are a million stars out tonight
swift satellites and grazing planets
strewn across that vault arched quiet
of a million stars
but your face bent above mine
is the solitary darkness
by which I feel most blessed.

The passions rise in this
in all new moon nights
slowly, surely
to a full brilliant circle
of rich hidden silver.

Thelki

Often in winter when the strands of self become undone
or in the depths of heat releasing summer
melting and wasting
all that the spiral of spring has accumulated
frequently
often
always in those times I yearn for the perfect place
vision of the heart
haven
home
the going-back-to
come-from place and
then I pick up walking stick
and head for the low roads
for whoever is lonely in the tribe of men who love men
is always remembering Thelki.

We swam though the major thoroughfare
clothes cast off
arching and gliding.
We swam through the shimmer
of meandering stream streets
city of beaches
houses clustered
aflutter
built on trees.

Thelki of a thousand fountains
shimmer of sun which is moon
a thousand man-dreams sparkling.

Ache of muscle
ache of fountain
arch of sky
arching back.

You rose beside me
arching up from the sea
you swam beside me
pearl shimmer cast into star-net
touching my hand
blue electric fire
searing the membrane of my intensity
your silver wet kiss
Thelki.

I have seen in the darkness
blue aching forms bent deep into the pulsing
I have seen in the silver blue arching forms
washed clean of the desiring and thus met
finally met
your fingers tracing the line of my lip
endlessly remembering
the electric shimmering.

I have tossed pearls from my back
only to dive again with you
into the rushing white water spray
then pull myself through mercury
racing you to the furthest end of the city.

There in the fountains
there in the heart of the mystery
there in the silver blue wet pulsing
there in the heart of the city
there I am blessed
we are blessed.

Thelki
baptismal
Thelki
washed clean
pure city
man city
half in and
half out
of dream.

Time

Eugene is waiting for Tom
Tom is waiting for José
José is waiting for Howard
Howard is still waiting for Kenji
Kenji is waiting
to finish his dissertation

Carlos is waiting for Tomas
Tomas is waiting for Sebastian
Sebastian is waiting for Renshu
Renshu is waiting for Vincent
Vincent is waiting for Walid
Walid is waiting for his thirtieth birthday

Time
waits for no man

Up Down Around:
Three Greek Tales

Up

Castor rolled a joint beneath a tree
while Nikos and Hector made out furiously
rolling in the grass and panting like dogs.

I sat next to the picnic basket
cutting slices of salami and finishing the wine
when the sky darkened
(there were no clouds that day)
what blocked the light
descended
fought off by myself and my friends
was an eagle with purple wings fifteen feet across.

Some trashy music was playing when I came to
on a gold-legged couch in a room whose walls were clouds
some swift hand had set and stilled into shapes
through which I could see out to a garden planted in the air.

"Where the hell am I?" I shouted
two slaves rushed in with food and clothing
"Olympus" one said, in a stoned-out voice
"Father Zeus" said the other, winking
"carried you here himself, Ganymede"
and left a purple plume as a love token on the night table.

"My parents will be worried sick."
Playing with a curl on my neck
Zeus said "They've been informed, dear"
pressing me beneath him with heavenly kisses

There are two heated pools, one indoors and one out
a sauna, gym, six tennis courts, and a private theatre
where you can watch anything you want.

They say Hera is insanely jealous
but perhaps because of my youth and womblessness
it was she who took my hand and led me from hall to hall
that, spiraling on clouds, collapse or grow at whims
"We haven't a ground plan, with everything changing.
Do you like your room? I picked it, specially."

He comes in the night, skin glowing
and slips into my bed, fragrant and tender
how could I have ever thought that Castor's kisses
were the height of bliss?

I've been working out in the gym
Poseidon's coaching me
Apollo teaching me to fly his two-seater
The hash here is fantastic.

Some nights he doesn't come
at first it bothered me that he has wives and lovers everywhere
but Athena said, "Look, Ganymede,
you're not only the only mortal Dad's brought up here,
but you're the only boy he's ever wanted."

Athena's always lending me books I never read
Zeus laughs when he sees them beside my bed
but just because I don't read doesn't mean I'm dumb
although he likes to think so
so I let him
cause it makes me seem sexier.

Aphrodite's probably my best friend
we liked each other right off
and I feel so comfortable with her
that I go to her refrigerator without asking
and she always has half a chocolate cake
or a cheese cake left over.

It's taken weeks for my ass to stop hurting
although I haven't said so
he's gentle but too big
which is funny cause when I was with Castor
I always wished he was bigger.

Dionysus wrote a play that we're all putting on
about some girl who becomes a junkie
and dies at her sister's wedding
Apollo is writing the music.

He's always bringing me things
gold sandals and a new robe
a pet penguin cause I saw one on TV
and said I liked it
it embarrasses me to take things
told him so
he said it's nothing to him
and besides I give him so much joy
just being here.

We were lying in bed eating grapes
I wondered what it would be like to make love in a mirror
suddenly the room transformed
into a mirrored sphere
he, kneeling between my legs
we, infinitely reflected.

Last week was birthday but I don't feel any older
Athena says it's like that here
Zeus gave me a new little palace of my own
Hera gave me a video recorder
Apollo gave me a tiny prop plane
Dionysus an electric piano
Hebe offered to give me lessons
I also got a surf board
a digital watch
a pocket calculator from Zephyr I think
we all smoked a lot and I mixed the cards up
the cake floated in by itself
wrapped in flames that didn't burn it
but took everyone's help to blow out.

Instead of racing off to a meeting
the next morning he stayed to have breakfast
fresh squeezed nectar and scrambled phoenix eggs
that afternoon he came to my bed
deep green gold iridescent
shimmering up the bedpost
fifty foot winged snake
once these things terrified me
now I say "Stop being silly, Zeus"
laughing as he changes into a sphinx, centipede, planet
himself.

He's the perfect lover
as the chief of the gods would have to be
each single hair an other hand caressing me.

That night he leaned above me
kissing my eyelids shut
then stretched out beside me
a moment later
my eyes opened to find that he'd transported us

food and all to a glass roofed pavilion
in the middle of a lunar crater
to watch the Earth rise
one side dipped in sunshine
green and brown and turning in white veils.

Hera says that Zeus is using me
that I run for his things like a slave
I laughed at her words and reminded her that
back home I worked in a pizza joint
waiting tables.

Last night he came to me
luminous turning eyes of fire
his triple-beating heart bent over mine
and whispered "Ganymede, my beautiful boy"
his touch electric and kisses better than the finest wine
but after he left me I whispered (to what god?)
that he who gives everything
when he kisses me in the night
with emerald eyes of shining fire
who can change himself into anything
and does
cloud
planet
sun
galaxy
cosmos
still cannot change himself
into someone
I can love.

Down

People still speak of our nuptials
the shining pavilion looking out on the sea
how my father King Oeagrus arrived in his limo

then my Muse mother Calliope and her eight sisters
in shimmering rainbow slippers
wind-colored robes.

The photographer zoomed in on Eurydice surrounded by
bridesmaids
barefoot with tinkling bells on their ankles
her dark hair pulled to one side and braided
with small white flowers
as down the path into the grotto she came toward me in my tuxedo
smiling.

The priestess wrapped ribbons around our hands
poured sweet wine at our feet
recited the ancient wedding chants
marrying Orpheus to Eurydice
as we held each other's hands
then I played the lyre and she danced.

Honey cakes, nut cakes
spiced bread on silver plates
iced grapes in glass bowls
ocean green
figs, dates.

Even today they speak of the Hollywood rock band
how Eurydice led the women
in a spiraling dance
around the pool and through the terraced garden
where she stumbled
bitten
by a serpent
hiding in the grass.

After her screaming stopped
hair, ribbons, gown, drooping over my arms

I carried her up the grotto path to the wedding suite.

Seven oil lamps burned above her head.
I wept
"How she loved you," her mother said,
sobbing on my back.

At the twelfth hour of darkness
I drew off Eurydice's grief-clinging mother
put sandals on and announced
with lyre in hand that I, a mortal but a Muse's son
would enter Hades' realm to bring back
my bride of one brief afternoon
and how her mother clung to me
painting kisses on my brow
"Yes, yes. With your lyre. If anyone can do it, you can."

What speaks of darkness better than Cerberus
Hell's three-headed guard
whose braying at obsidian gate
stills any heart that hasn't been killed yet.
I plucked my lyre
fingers moving on strings in a butterfly dance
that silenced Hell's vicious guardian
then I slipped into the frigid cavern
following amber neon arrows
pointing toward the seat of power.

"Who," great Hades bellowed
as I approached his throne
his stolen diamond queen beside him
"Who still living dares to enter Hell?"

Trembling
palms damp
I plucked my lyre

opening up to the spiraling notes
washing through me.

First Persephone, clutching a string of black pearls
then he
as I stroked their inner feelings
smiled and I sang
the song of a grief-struck mountain
cloven on his wedding day
from she whose smile awakens flowers.

She bent and whispered to him
let fall a tear
he summoned a guard who vanished and reappeared
spiked wings locked round a vapor-clad Eurydice.

"Go quickly," he said
"Do not look back."
We fled as he rose
the night queen clutching his cold hand.

Her footsteps did not echo as we ran
past the security cameras
only the whisper of my name
only the chill behind me
only the smell of dying flowers
let me know that she was there.

Eurydice
as the light in the far distance
up the boulder strewn path
steep, treacherous
entered, diffused
as a halted dawn might be
Eurydice
the moment I turned to see you

you fell back into the night
pulled as leaf is pulled
into a whirlpool.

In her parents' house
pierced sounds of mourning
for the twice-dead bride
"No one," her mother said
"can blame himself
for failing the impossible."

How many years have I wandered
two-shadowed, inconsolable
lyre my only companion
among the rocky hills of Thrace
where trees incline
drip sap
boulders cold and pressed together
lions, when I play
curl up with dogs
and the forest weeps for me
"Orpheus, Orpheus
release this needless pain
as incense burns yet freely gives its scent."
I try but guilt has sealed my inward tomb.

One night
the followers of Dionysus surrounded me
screaming "Never the day"
frenzied and bloodied
"Never the day
that a man's lies go unpunished"
knowing what I've never dared to whisper
even to my shrink.

Eurydice

I bleed
who will join you in the darkness very soon
and finally say
that I turned back to see you
hoping
you would not be there
or be turned
my twice-rejected bride
into
my
longed for
dreamed for
groom

Around

"Why don't I have a father like everyone else?"
Theseus asked at breakfast.
Aethra had been waiting for that question
pushed a silver bowl across the table
"Have some more oatmeal."

He'd just turned sixteen
never had acne and although he hadn't yet begun to shave
was smoothly muscled and in good form from throwing the discus
in the park with friends after school.
"How time flies"
Aethra sighed to herself
watching the throb of muscle in his tawny arm.

"Aegeus left us when you were an infant
and returned to Athens
after his own father died.
He is king there."
Theseus put an arm around his wet-eyed mother
not asking why this father didn't take them along.
Later she gave him

the jeweled knife he'd left behind.

"I think it's a mistake" his therapist said
removing his glasses
"to be leaving now, when you're making so much
progress, but I understand your need to go
to Athens, and I wish you great success on your trip."

At the dinner table his mother began to sob
"I don't like the idea of his hitching to Athens"
she appealed to Pittheus her father
but Theseus had already stuffed his pack
which stood near the umbrella stand.
A fast wink passed from grandfather to grandson
"I understand your fears, Aethra
but Theseus is quite a young man now
and I think this trip is exactly what he needs."
A slave brought in a huge good-bye cake
covered with mounds of whipped cream and strawberries
Aethra had one glass too many of white wine
and told Theseus how she'd met his father.

At sunrise, before Aethra was up
Pittheus drove Theseus down to the freeway
hugged him and said "I believe in you boy."
They both cried.

The sun was hot as cars sped by
Theseus had a knot in his stomach
bigger than the day he started high school
His pack pulled him down
"Maybe I should stand closer to the on-ramp"
Towards noon (he waited that long)
a shiny white Vega slowed up with windows rolled down
"Which way you going?"
"To Athens."

"So am I."

The city appeared suddenly above them
a thousand opals
Theseus gulped
pulled out the pencil directions his mother gave
and walked the rest of the way.

"King's House
Guided Tours"
the sign read on a white stone wall
a small side door and a ticket line
"You'll have to check that"
clerk nodding at his pack
the guard laughed when Theseus said
"I'm Aegeus's son"
"And I'm Zeus's son, kid
just check your pack."
Theseus reached into it
pulled out Aegeus's knife
wrapped in three pairs of socks.
The guards wrestled him to the ground.

Later Aegeus sat laughing on his throne
turning the jewel-encrusted knife in his hand
watching the glitter of his name worked in in topaz
then looked up proudly at the fine lines of his son
"My nose and chin."

Theseus texted later to his grandfather
"Dad is tall and looks young for his age
he's so much like me, and I like him."
Pittheus skipped that last part when he read it to his daughter.

Each day Theseus and Aegeus would go
riding or hunting or work out in the gymnasium

at night there were huge banquets
when all Athens in tuxedoes and gowns
turned out to meet their handsome future king
"He's gorgeous."
"The very image of his father."
"He *is* talking to Niobe."
"Did you see him dance?"

There was a strange feeling in the palace
vague, misty, indefinable
one afternoon out on the terrace
the two of them eating lunch together
Theseus plucked up his nerve
and asked about it
Aegeus frowned and put his fork down.
"I should have told you sooner
but this is the time of year
when we're forced to pay human tribute
to the king of Crete."

The plot evolved slowly in his mind without first telling his father
who flew up from the table overturning his plate.
"What, loose you to Minos? Now that I've finally got you!"
In the end we know that Aegeus was finally persuaded.

The ship set out with black sails for Crete
carrying fourteen of Athens' most beautiful youths and maidens
from all the best families
standing at the dock but no one waving.

Theseus had spent hours in conference
with his father's secret service men
and as the salt sea winds blew over the deck he sat by himself
reviewing their information
thinking of all the good times he'd had in Athens
thinking well of even his stepmother Medea

deciding to bring back a bracelet or necklace from Crete
watching the froth of wake break into sparklettes behind the ship.

At night below deck they plotted
"Our spies are in contact with Ariadne the king's daughter
with her help we cannot fail."
a youth played lyre so the crew could not hear
as moon rose amber from pink sea.

Long last morning
noon
Crete appeared on the horizon
approached slowly
towns strewn green and red and white
as the markings on the back of a water snake
they docked in the harbor
black among pastel and lay there all evening.

Morning after eating
they were ferried to shore, to the docks
to the edge of a terraced garden city
tossed like a veil among the trees.
"Easy to escape here."

Feasted daily as such captives always are
left to wander trickling-fountain courtyards
bird fish vine painted suites
Ariadne sent a baked hen to Theseus
with Daedalus's labyrinth blueprints
wrapped in tin foil in the stuffing.

Elegant hand
fine lines
the plan of the labyrinth
long halls
circuitous passageways

steeply inclined stairs
narrow airshafts
spiraling in
on the den
the hidden nest
of the minotaur.

On their last night a basket of wax fruit was delivered
Theseus split them all till he found a note in a lemon
a ball of string in an orange
and a small silver pistol slipped inside a pineapple
no one could sleep but
painted, jeweled they sat in their tight Cretan finery
on elegant chairs
watching a sappy romance movie.

Dawn came over the hill
fat yellow fist
the captain of the king's guard
ten priestesses
a throng of sistrum-playing eunuchs led the flowered
red-eyed captives toward the labyrinth.

Painted in Dedalus's hand above the heavy bronze doors
"This I have built out of my dreaming
for someone else's nightmare."
Words already fading
a radio playing somewhere as they disappeared one by one
into the darkness.

Long pink marble lobby floor
arched ceiling and flower-papered walls
lit by dim shaded lamps placed every few feet
Theseus found the dimmer switch and turned them up
told his fourteen companions to hold one end of the string
and wait by the door for him.

Down long dim halls that bent into false turns
back up long dark corridors
opening onto a Louis Seize salon
a Bauhaus living room
nibbling on candy from silver or cut-glass bowls
looking for a bathroom
no windows or false, thick-curtained ones only.

The ball of string grew smaller and smaller
as he moved, cautiously
sometimes in circles
anxious
exhausted.

The marble foyer
the sleek curves of the walls
black and white Doric pillars
according to the floor plan
this was the entry
to the minotaur's apartment.

Silent
but for the drone of central air
and the distant echo
of an old Cole Porter song
Theseus stared at himself in a mirror
seeming to grow older as the minutes passed
combed his ruddy hair out of his eyes
paced with hands thrust in back pockets
a tub ran down the hall
silently he inched his way slowly toward double white doors
into lime green room ringed by dark green curtains and settees.

A narrow hall led to the bedroom
Theseus stopped

music silenced
no movement behind the door
waiting
the squeak of mattress
silence
a sigh soft breathing.

He turned the door handle
gold plated
pistol in his other hand
pushed open the door
just as the string ran out.

Across the room on a low raised bed
pink sheets tossed
soft pillows
dark curls
lay the dark sprawled minotaur.

Theseus froze
bathed in light from the hall
the minotaur
one leg bent
on his back
scarlet horns on the pillow
broad hairy chest gently rising and falling
Theseus took a step closer
hands clenched
the minotaur leaped up
grabbed his own pearl-handled revolver
from the night table next to his rumpled bed
eyes met
he dropped the gun
as Theseus approached
on path
their eyes had cut.

Where lips have met of strangers
so unstrange
where arms and hearts
have long dreamed of each other
now
finally
met
I draw the curtain
but to say
that damp moist forest
rose upon itself
to forest meet that night
of pleasured wealth.

Morning by the clock
found two dark forms entwined on bed
shirt jeans shoes socks tossed on floor
tossed on a wave of pinkness.

In the next room an automatic espresso machine
began to rumble and a radio and the lights
tucked in behind moldings
came on slowly.

It did not seem unreasonable
in a world where gods
disguised as birds or snakes
would slip down for extramarital affairs
that two men
after one short long deep night
of loving
might begin to make plans
over coffee and eggs
feet caressing beneath the table.

There were certain moments when Theseus
who was not very experienced in matters of love
found it impossible to believe
that someone as beautiful as the minotuar
who for years had slept with
(and then devoured)
endless captives of both sexes
from cities all over the Mediterranean
could love him
and for the minotaur
there were moments when their eyes met
and he found it impossible to believe that someone so good
so pure as Theseus
so innocent and so lovely
could love in return a wild beast of a man
with all his sordid history –
but he did.

And here our tale ends.

String Duet

I played you like a violin
Stradivarius
ancient
tongue and fingers
moving through your strings

You did not
play me

You did not
even listen

Family Portrait

We too are a people
As ancient as dawn
Who have no homeland
We come from the stars
All homes are ours
For where we are needed
Is where we are born.

In the song of all songs
We too have a chorus
Timeless, long, beautiful
Wherever we sing it
For we are a people of music
Always have been
Singing to the world.

Are we not dancers
In every temple we create
From cellar to grove
Pillared hall to grave
Dancing the wonder of life
For all to see
The heart dance of love
That created the cosmos
Oneness, giving birth to all and everything
And we
The sacred priests of Oneness
Dancing.

We are the balancers
Walk-Betweens
The healers
Of all who are in need

Of woman and man
Of old and young
Of the living and the dying
Of the birthing and the dead
Ours are the weaving hands
That heal and bind the world together.

In between and at cliff edge
We stand
Peering out into the future
For we are a scouting people
Scouting for all the people
Seeking life
Seeking truth
Seeking purpose
Seeking dreams.

We are the guardians of the trees
Priests of Father Earth
Rainbow dancers
Gatekeepers
Joy masters
Bridge builders
And makers of beauty
Beauty for every other tribe
Coming from them all
We are weavers of desire.

We are an ancient people
Walking the crack of dusk
Of dawn
We have no homeland
We come from the stars
All lands are ours
For we are born
Wherever we are needed.

Want

I want to touch you,
face half-lit by moon.

I want to touch you,
hands clenched at your side.

I want to touch you,
bed strewn thistle deep.

I want to touch you.
No bird sings.

Song of the Great God Dimawadi to His Beloved Nimiway

Sung in the cities of Umurru
in the streets and taverns
sung to string and wooden flutes
this is the love song the great god Dimawadi
sang to his beloved Nimiway
sang to flutes and ringing instruments
in the cities of Umurru
in the house of his beloved Nimiway.

It is I who sing
the great god Dimawadi
who descended from the heavens
to take on flesh
it is I who sing now, Dimawadi
ruler of Umurru
come from heaven.

Great is my name among the people
loudly they praise me
Dimawadi Dimawadi Dimawadi
ruler of the city and master of the sea.

Ten thousand sheep they bring me
rams, ewes,
bound, unblemished
sheep they bring me
cattle and unguents and spices they bring
woven clothes
precious stones
to my house
my temple

great house of Dimawadi
doors covered with gold
whose towers shine
high above the city.

It is I who created the cities
it is I who made the canals
built high the gates and walls
took on flesh to walk among the people
took on flesh
to dance with you Nimiway
Nimiway son of Bilitu
Bilitu the princess of the mountains
your lips I took on flesh to meet
your limbs rubbed smooth with scented oils
gentle you reached a trembling hand to me
and we danced together in the moonlight
and I held you and rocked you
in the night in your bed
while the oil lamps flickered.

Yes I came down and stayed
I came down from the heavens
and I stayed with you
I took on flesh
I descended from the clouds
I took on flesh
to answer the call of one who
already loved me
yes I came down
I came down from on high
from the house of our Holy Mother Sky
I took on flesh
I came to your house Nimiway
I came to your bed.

And this is the song that I sing
this is the love song of the god Dimawadi
this is the song the great god sings
to the sound of gold flutes
in my garden
standing beneath the vines
having come here to love
come here to dance
come here to sing to you
Nimiway son of Bilitu
noble princess of the mountains
beloved of the great god Dimawadi
first of the gods to walk on earth.
yes
this is the song that I sing to you
sing to you
Nimiway son of Bilitu
in the city of Umurru
in our garden
on the morning
of our wedding.

Dancing

I am standing in a crowded smoke-filled room
my back to the wall. The music is blasting, and
he, my first boyfriend, is dancing with someone else,
their tight shirts wet and clinging to their torsos.

I was told in elementary school that I could not sing
because of the annoying vibrato in my voice,
and being pigeon-toed, unable to skate,
constantly tripping over my own two feet,
I was told that I could never dance.

He is dark and beautiful, curly of hair and
handsome behind his Coke-bottle glasses.
We are the same size in everything but shoes
and being poor college students, we have
between us only one set of clothes.

The band members are sexy in
a slightly older bearded hippie way
and how the hunky guitarist clutches
his instrument tells us everything
about their music. Hot. But
my eyes are focused on my boyfriend
gyrating and moving upright much
as he moves with me in bed, horizontal.

Transfixed by his body I do not see
an older man coming right toward me
who reaches out and grabs my hand and
says as he pulls me into the crowd
"Honey, all fags can dance!"

We noticed him when we came in, maybe
in his forties, oldest man in the room. And now
he is wrapped around me, sweaty, pressed to my
chest and pulling up in me some form of pure free
movement in my body that I did not ever know existed.
Or had forgotten, so many years since I used to dance
wildly in the living room to the symphonies of
Beethoven, till I grew afraid that my brother would walk
in on me one afternoon and sneer. So I stopped.

When the song is done, when I have been moving with him,
hot now and alive, he pushes me away and toward my
boyfriend, who has been watching with disbelief,
he will tell me later,
having tried to get me to dance with him several times before.

In his arms what has risen up in me is on fire, liquid fire, and
my fire meets his fire, and the rhythm that surges through the
room has taken over our bodies, and we move in a way that I
have never moved before, heart to heart and pumping pulsing
pressing hard cocks into each other's body till we burn the
club down, second floor somewhere on Polk Street, San
Francisco, early spring of 1973.

Indug the Triumphant

Indug the sorrowful
Indug the traveler
charter of galaxies
maker of star maps.

At the heart of his crystal ship he sits
soft pads of fingers poised above the cold controls
empty and questing
fierce with himself
saying "Indug Indug Indug
you warp your way across the cosmos
like a bird migrating
to a thousand stellar homes
oh Indug
remember the time you nearly died between stars
on warp-break and the time
swift-chased by Zellar's hungry astro-pirates
pursued between stars
again you nearly died."

Oh Indug
who sought and found
the furthest star at the edge of the universe
Indug pull yourself together
heat of finger pressing the warp-button
bursting your star ship across the grid of space-time
in a fraction of an instant plunging into
momentary non-existence sixty light-years away
in pure warp, pure leap, pure orgasm
in/out, being/non
Indug Indug Indug
give up this craziness
madness

space fever
dream sickness.

Indug traveled
he traveled the stars
he traveled the stars to escape a dream
a dream that awakened him
Indug traveled to worlds, planets, stars
to escape
escape the dream
the night and waking dreams
that held onto him.

On Suhlran
he saw a hand in the marketplace
a waving hand
but it was not his
and he fled again.

In a space café
orbiting above the poison clouds of O-e-o
on the walk-ramp he saw a man
from the back with a mane of hair
a shining mane of aqua hair
but it was not him.

On Mahataq
in a lobby down a hallway talking
he saw a man in a caftan, face half-turned
saw nose and ears and horns
then eyes he saw
but it was not him
was not him
and he flew and he fled
and had that night his dream again.

Weary of fleeing
tired of wandering
in his crystal cosmic traveling ship
he turns around
warps around
warp-jumps
the galaxy
like skimming pebble
midnight pond
goes back home to Karcan
where he knows that he will find him.

To the outermost court
of the house of Jamuti
Jamuti his once beloved
the stone house
the jeweled house
of Jamuti
the consul of Sharr.

And the servants
the strong and able servants
remember him
and the valet
old and loyal
remembers Indug
remembers his pain
remembers saying
"Jamuti doesn't let anyone get close to him"
in the morning in the great hall
under glass ceiling
beneath a rosy sun
and now he leads him to the garden
leads Indug to Jamuti's garden.

Indug waits

paces
beneath the massive kwarr tree's
quivering orange leaves
till Jamuti appears
out a long dark hallway
Jamuti the once and still beloved
his mane of aqua hair
gone and the flare
of his arched cheekbones collapsed
but his shining horns
the same
eyes of amber fire the same
and his five knuckled
six fingered hands
tremble as Jamuti
reaches out to Indug
strokes his indigo face.

"Oh Indug
hero of stars
your exploits I have followed
your travels
and now you are home again
back to find me old and fallen
who cast you off so long ago
oh Indug
so many the nights I dreamt of your bright eyes
shining at me
and now the sky has brought you back."

They step closer
pause
wait
hearts dancing up through
silver sparkling eyes
then reach out

trembling
remembering hands
six-fingered
elegant
and embrace
caress
sing
dance
re-dance
kiss
as first
the pearl
then the opalescent
moons
rise
shining
full
and touch
      above
the peaked

          horizon.

We Have Made the Seasons

We have made the seasons in our bed
knocking hard as winter branches
joint to joint and bone to bone revealed.

Snow covered first chilled connection
thaw breaking
spring trickle unleashed beneath arms
back cleft
across the green
pressing up flowers to the sun of each
bringing the heat on
touching deep beneath skin
flesh melting
damp sheet encumbered
cast away.

Who run with hands mouth legs
groping for islands and splashing deep into waves
to the source, the breath
breathless
where gather puddles
damp leaf musk smell.

The Man with the Moon
Over His Shoulder

You captured me across the wires.
There is death in your voice.
Gulls, shattered glass, raging fire.

Where is he, where is he, where is he?
The man with the moon over his shoulder.
Some men come draped in leather, muscle, rust.
But he will come tender bathed in soft wet silver
chalice, grail, cup bearing
sweet open lips saying "Drink. Please drink with me."

In the dark, in the deep of night
some turn to dreams of lust, of power.
But he, soft as a forest, whispers "Come. Come walk with me,"
smooth open hand leading down across the mossy wet night
to river-sigh places where feet curl over stones
worn smooth in the wash of time's desire.

Spring bubbling
hair curling
fern damp
palm wet on my back
body falling, body rising
breath singing, breath crying.

You cut me with your eye.
You prowl.
Your face is a searchlight
looking for something
you seem to not be able to find.

Where is he, where is he?
The man with the moon
over his shoulder.
In my dream his eyes are closed
as he sleeps beside me.
On whose heaven-beam shoulders
hang stars like a mobile
herbs, dried on the rafters, in the attic, under skylight
each leaf, each table, our bed.
Slipping soft
like suede, like glove, luminous.

And he turns to me
palm damp
upturned to me as I watch him sleeping.
Chest rising and falling, slow as the tide on a landless world.
In the dark, in the drowning
where flesh, unhinged, is born from the ache, the rub
that kindles new stars
and whispers on silver that floods
from the ancient dark rising deep lunar blood.

I have seen him briefly in the eyes of some
the hands, the kisses of men who touch.
O silver that floods from the deep
from the sighs
from the ancient deep root of men.
Rock.
Stone.
The twin dark mountains worn smooth by river.
Smooth as a fawn's skin weeping and birthing the joy dance.

Where is he, where is he, where is he?
The man with the moon in his hair
who trembles and touches and rocks in the night
there beside me, holding me

emptied, in my arms, of fierceness, of anger.

He walks with his head held high
the oak of his back straight as morning
and his hands know softness and he sees with an eye
that touches all things, each eye a finger
pressed close to flower, to bark
pressed close over me.

Where is he?
The man with the moon in his soul
who turns in a dance
his face, now child, now ancient
wearing sorrow and pain
lit by the heart and the laughter
and the sweet glad living joy refrain
of river-wet bodies mingling.

Where is he
where is he
where is he
where is he?
The man with the moon slung over his shoulder?
Who holds me and turns me
and dreams new worlds
where is he
where is he
where is he
where is he
new moon pressed on his shoulder
a nibble, a kiss, a sigh
tattooed on his soul.
Whose face
now laughing, now ancient
now child, now ocean
rises up, washes up, races through me.

In the flicker of morning
in the birthing of blueness.

Where is he
Where is he
Where is he
Where is he
Where is he?

At the Golden Gate Bridge

Once
there was only water
flowing between land and land
not metal
no
not metal span
nor cars nor trucks nor buses
just water flowing
between here and there.

And yet
and yet
and yet
standing here now
on the edge of traffic
I can feel
the arched connection
that was always here
like we are
men who love men
born into every family
walking across
what sometimes
divides others
but for us
is flowing
homeward
always
here
long before
we were even dreamed of.

In the Sacred Forest

You echo my limbs

beneath this sacred tree.
and answer my prayers
at the height of
summer's green-fire.

You echo my song
beneath a cloudless sky
and all the world
hovers
motionless
in the space
between
our
shining
bodies.

Wingsong

I carry you on my back
I carry every one of you
who has died
on my back.

You are not a burden
your weight is exalting
each one of you
is another feather
in my arched wings.

You carry me
every one of you
carries me higher and higher
into my life
into the physical life
I live
for every one of you.

When I sleep, you sleep too
when I dance, you dance too
when I pray, you are praying with me
and every time I kiss another man
each one of you
pressed up behind my lips
is drinking too
swan, hummingbird, egret, eagle
drinking.

I drink for all of you
I live with all of you
together, together, together,
all of us are

drinking
living
dancing
flying.

The Song of Father Earth

You are invited to imagine:
4 speakers, 4 dancers, and projected images of the planet.

Something is wrong here *(Each line is spoken by a different speaker)*
something painful *(Dancers begin to move silently across the stage
        of your mind)*
I do not want to read the news
because something is very wrong here
a good friend calls in tears
the air is bad
a cousin is dying

And a deep lament rises up now in our dreams
awakening us to ancient memories . . . .
of how things were for more than one hundred thousand years
before we called Earth mother
when still we called sky
Mother, Creator, Holy Only God

Deep ancient memories collide
with the wrongs that we have done . . . .
in the ways we've been living
and yet
in spite of all that we have done
to harm you . . . . . *(Each refrain is chanted by all 4 speakers)*

Your body is beautiful
Father Earth.
Hard and strong and powerful
ancient, fertile, soft, wet, living.

And though we have forsaken you

defiled you
ignored your father-limits
leveled your sacred forest groves
exterminated your creatures
misaligned your seasons . . .

Your body is beautiful
Father Earth.
Hard and strong and powerful
ancient, fertile, soft, wet, living.

Smokestacks, train tracks
cars on endless highways
our lauded factories pour forth toxins
that poison all that lives here
and we
and we
are poisoned too
and yet . . . .

Your body is beautiful
Father Earth.
Hard and strong and powerful
ancient, fertile, soft, wet, living.

We did not listen
took what was not ours to take
stole, cut, dug, burned, raped
your sacred ancient living body
without listening to your many many warnings
and still . . .

Your body is beautiful
Father Earth.
Hard and strong and powerful
ancient, fertile, soft, wet, living.

Birds – dying.
trees – dying.
we ourselves – all slowly dying
from what we have done
and yet . . .

Your body is beautiful
Father Earth.
Hard and strong and powerful
ancient, fertile, soft, wet, living.

And this is the song
of our great remembering
before it is too late
we stop
we stop
we awaken.
and remember that . . . .

Your body is beautiful
Father Earth.
Hard and strong and powerful
ancient, fertile, soft, wet, living.

Sea-washed
land-swept
sky-haloed
life-haven

(all on stage stop moving and the images are no longer projected)

Holy your body
holy your streams, rivers, oceans.
holy your forests.
holy the life still growing up from you.

and as we remember this
act from it
all becomes holy holy holy once again.

And this is the song of Father Earth
this is the song of salvation
sung in this sacred time
of holy dedication
to
You   *(shouted by all on stage)*
You   *(whispered by all on stage)*
You   *(mouthed by all on stage)*
You   *(as they place their hands over their heart,*
         and then bow downward,
         slowly lowering their hands
         to the ground
         with their fingers pointing
         toward the audience)

The Comfort of Aging

This old world, that moon
constant, even in the day
cut, mended, turning, returning.

The paper talks of war
and climate change
a fire raging in the West
the high price
of prescription medication.

And this old world, that moon
silver, pockmarked, hazy.

The dull pain in my lower back
another dear friend's death
my old bald head and aching hip
and down the street
the gutted homeless camp.

And that old moon, this world
stone hard and constant
comfort me now
as I did not know
how to let them do
when I was twenty-five.

Ritual for Walks-Between Gatherings

To be read by one to all who are gathered together in a circle, or to read by all to all, each man reading another paragraph, sitting or standing, as your gathering chooses.

WE ARE AN ANCIENT people. Because we live between male and female, matter and spirit, the living and the dead, and because we come from all other peoples, we were and are honored in many cultures for our capacity to link, connect, and unify. We have been called gatekeepers and bridge builders. We are the Walks-Between People, a natural healing and peacekeeping force in the world.

As consciousness scouts we explore the terrain of the life to find what is new and needed. We are transformational artists and beauty-makers. We are healers, especially gifted as midwives for the dying. We have always met in sacred groves, for we are the guardians of the trees, a vital role at this time. Some of us work alone, others in community. Sometime we work through our actions, and sometimes we work silently, in prayer and meditation. Now is the time for us to fully own who we are, as individuals and as a tribe, in a world that sorely needs our gifts.

Gathered together in this circle, feel the river of life that runs through us all. Holding hands, slowly look and feel your way around the circle as you are able, into the eyes of every other man, and let yourself be looked at and deeply into, feeling the energy that begins to rise up in your body, in our bodies. Touching your feet to the feet of the man standing or sitting beside you, feel the way that we are rooted together, grounded together, like the living breathing walking trees we are.

Now, with feet still touching, bring both your hands to your chest for a moment, close your eyes and feel your breath and your heartbeat.

Open your eyes again and slowly rub your body from head to toe, wherever you can reach. Put your right hand on your abdomen, between your navel and pubic bone, and say out loud, "We are a sacred people." Notice where you feel sacred in your body and mind, and where you don't. Continuing to inhale and exhale, breathe sacredness into every part of your body, for we are priests of Father Earth and Mother Sky.

Lower your right hand. Put your left hand on your heart and say, "We are a healing tribe." Notice where you feel the power of healing in your body and mind and where you don't. Gently breathe healing into every part of who you are, for we are the Hand Tribe, innately blessed with the gift of sacred touch. At the core of our gifts is our capacity for healing and renewal, for ourselves and for all the world.

Keep your left hand on your heart and place your right hand on your abdomen again. Feel the energy that begins to spiral between both hands, filling your body. Send this energy down through your feet to the living body of Father Earth, and out through the top of your head into the vastness of Mother Sky. Now, breathe in both their energies, down through the top of your head and up through the bottoms of your feet, feeling them merge in your body. Be conscious of your own sacred tasks and the ways that you can manifest them in the world.

Now, join hands again, with your feet still touching the feet of the man sitting or standing beside you. Feel the power of the circle growing, as it moves through each one of us and spreads out beyond our bodies, and now let us say out loud to each other, "We are a sacred people. We are a healing tribe." Then inhale deeply and with a strong slow exhalation, feel that the energy of this circle connects all of us who are gathered together, blessing us in our holy chosen bodies.

Now, let us turn so that we are facing outward, with our backs to each other. Join hands and touch feet again, and inhale and exhale deeply. And just as a pebble tossed into a lake sends out ripples, let us send our healing and loving energy out to all of the men in our tribe, wherever they are in the world, letting them know that they are not alone, ever, for we are with them, and all of us are one tribe joined together.

With hands and feet connected, and connected with our sacred brothers everywhere, let us inhale slowly, and as we slowly exhale let us send out another wave of energy to the people in any troubled places in the world. Know that the energy of our tribe is helping to transform the world, in ways that emerge from who we are and always have been, as men who love men, as the Walks-Between People.

Still connected, let us send out another wave of energy to all the pregnant women in the world, that they be blessed and that the children they are carrying be blessed. Some of those children are the incoming men of our tribe, and the ripple of energy we send out to them will let them know that they are holy and will be met and welcomed and cared for and protected by us when they arrive.

Now send out energy to everyone in the world, knowing as we do so that the energy of our tribe is helping to transform the world, in ways that emerge from who we are and always have been, as men who love men. For we are a Walks-Between People. A bridge-making people. And now is the time for us to do our work in the world.

Inhaling and exhaling, slowly and deeply, as each of us feels called to, let us send energy out to all the plants and animals, who are so in need of healing from the damage we have done to them. And ask them to forgive us and work with us as we move by our actions to heal the world.

Turn back to face the others in our circle, joining hands and touching feet again. Now look around the circle. Feel the way that we are connected from body to body, from hand to hand, from foot to foot. Inhale. Exhale. Now bring your hands back to your abdomen and heart, and slowly whisper to each other, "We are a sacred people. We are a healing tribe. We are wise and strong and loving. We are here to change the world."

As the vibration of those words ripples out into shared silence, feel that the energy generated in our circle is spreading out around the planet, to rivers and mountains, to oceans and continents, spreading down to the center of the planet and out to the edge of the atmosphere, shining out and down into the sacred body of the living planet itself – Father Earth. And let us send our energy out beyond our home world, out into solar system, galaxy, out into the universe, and out and out beyond it so that it shimmers in every cell of the body of our timeless Mother Sky.

Now let us slowly begin to move in our circle, as we are able, remaining in silence, for I have been told the religion of the future will be a global faith of silent dancing. So dance now, sacred brothers, holy family, joined together in a circle. Let the energies of Father Earth and Mother Sky fill us and move us and turn and enliven us, light and love shining out from our sacred bodies.

The leader or leaders wait till the energy and movement
that's risen up has begun to slow down,
and then the final speaker speaks.

Now as the energy settles down again, stills itself as it moves through us, let us come back to stillness, sitting or standing together. Feeling our breath rising and falling in our blessed and blessing bodies, let us look around the circle again, feel our way around the circle again, deeply into each other's heart.

Let us bow to each other. And take this energy with us as we step apart.

When I Died

FOUR TIMES I'VE DREAMT about my death. The first two dreams were exactly the same. I'm a very old man, propped up on pillows in a big bed, beneath a white bedspread, in a room with white walls, a white dresser. Four or five of my students are with me, sitting on the edges of the bed, or beside it in white chairs. To my left, on a plate, is a cheesecake, to my right is a bowl of fruit. Across from me is an open window with white curtains pulled back. Out the window – an apple orchard. All of us are talking, I drift off to sleep. The next thing I know – I'm standing in the wall behind the bed, watching my students, all in their twenties and thirties, slowly discover that I'm dead. They begin to get upset and I beam out to them a loud telepathic message: "I thought I taught you better than this. I'm still here, standing in the wall. Turn around and notice."

Twice I had that dream. The third time I had it, everything was exactly the same – the room, the sequence of events, my students – except that instead of being white, the walls, dresser, bedspread, chairs, curtains, were all a warm lovely yellow. And I remember a night, years after I had those dreams. The moon was full and I was walking through an apple orchard behind the five-hundred-year-old farm house I was teaching at, staying in, in a tiny town in Germany, Klein Sachau. The orchard looked very like the one in my dream and I thought, "How odd. How unlikely." For I was born in Germany in the life before this one, and it was in a gas chamber that I died, a six-year-old Jewish boy. But that's a whole other story, for a whole other time.

In all three of those dreams I was alert, a bit frail, and older than I ever thought I'd live to be, as my father died two days after his fifty-seventh birthday, and my mother died at seventy-four, six months short of one of her big life goals: to see the year 2000. But in those dreams I was very old. And old is important because when I was a boy, my mother, exasperated that all I wanted to do was stay in my bedroom and read, used to snap, "What's wrong with you?

Living with you is like living with an eighty-six-year-old man." Her
words made me want to live to be at least eight-seven, so that I
could find out what she meant.

The fourth dream was different.

I am walking through a beautiful cemetery. It's early summer.
The trees are heavy with emerald-dark leaves. All at once I come
upon a very large headstone, almost a foot thick and as wide as the
headboard of a queen-size bed. The stone is a dark brownish-grey,
flecked and sparkling in the slanting light. Three thoughts come to
me simultaneously, as I read the words carved into the stone:

Andrew Ramer
March 24, 1951—September 15, 2063

One – Wow, I lived a long time.
Two – I must have accomplished something in this life, to merit
such a great big stone.
Three – It's so plain. I don't really like it. No epitaph. And not a
single decoration.

Disappointed, I woke up.

And I think of that dream now, having decided when I turned
seventy this March to start going by the middle name that my
companion angel gave me in 1988 – Elias – the name of my Italian
Jewish paternal great great grandfather. Or so my father's father
told me, right before my bar mitzvah. And I wonder – will Elias
Ramer live as long as Andrew Ramer? Die sooner? Or live for even
longer?

My Hebrew name is Shabtai, which I share with my maternal
great great great grandfather and also with my maternal great
grandfather Alexander, who Andrew was named after. The second
Shabtai was born in Russia in 1870 and died in Brooklyn in 1950.
The first Shabtai was born in the Caucasus in the 1700s and died
in the Crimea in the 1900s, when he was 137 years old. Or so the
family story goes.

And so, I go. One hundred and fifty-five pounds, as I have been for decades. Bald for far longer than I had hair on my head. White of beard and mustache. Chest and ears hairier than they used to be, but the hair in my armpits and legs long gone, seventy years after I arrived. Still wrapped in a yellow blanket. Moving toward death. Perhaps in a sunny yellow room, looking out on an apple orchard. But here, for now. On a cool spring night in 2021. Still a walker. (More than 2000 miles last year.) Rememberer. And a teller of the stories of our people. That no one else can tell, but one of our people.

Acknowledgments

For the cover art

Deep gratitude to Michael Starkman, whose luminous creation blesses the cover of this book. And thank you for the dance we've been doing since we met all those years ago in New York. When I finished the first draft of *Two Flutes Playing* I made four copies and gave one to you. You gave it to Larry Hermsen, who gave it to Joseph Kramer who published the first edition in 1990, for which I thank you. To see more of Michael's luminous images go to – michaelstarkman.com

For the outward

Thank you Bo, Trebor, Toby, Will, and Franklin – masterful writers and visionaries all – for your wonderful words of blessing. To meet their marvelous work go to:

- www.whitecraneinstitute.org
- http://treborhealey.com/
- http://www.tobyjohnson.com/
- https://www.willsworld.org
- www.tenminutemuse.wordpress.com

Aᴄᴋɴᴏᴡʟᴇᴅɢᴍᴇɴᴛꜱ

For the Foreword

Thank you Don Shewey for your entrance to this book through the portal of your luminously gorgeous words. I am moved and delighted, and also thank you for introducing me to Jonathan. You will be able to meet Don's own wonderful writing when you visit - www.donshewey.com

For the inward

Thank you Jonathan Mack, for bringing your writer's eyes, ears, and heart to this book. You will discover some of Jonathan's marvelous word at - www.patreon.com/JonathanMack

For "Stories of Our People"

This part of the book began in Brooklyn in the late 1980s when my friend Prue See and I were going off to hear Johnny Moses, the Pacific Northwest Native American storyteller. On the way down the stairs to meet Prue, like lightning I was struck by "A Story of our People," which I wrote down when I got to the bottom of the stairs. (Some people always carry a pad in their backpack.) Thank you Prue and thank you Johnny!

All the rest of these stories exist because of Raven Wolfdancer. In addition to being the creator of the images for them, and the muse for their unfolding, Raven (1946-1993) was a community activist, gardener, Earth-lover, poet, musician, and a Native American pipe carrier. I'm in awe of his drawings. They're mystical, sensual, expansive, and surreal. There is time in a story, as long as it takes to tell. But in Raven's drawings – eternity is flowing. Flow with it. Be with it. Take it into your heart and your life. In doing so, you will complete the drawings that Raven did not live to draw, who had one foot in another world when he was doing them.

Although several of them are no longer with us, this part of the book was nourished by the friendship and visions of Barbara Shor, Charles Lawrence, Carol Robin, Bonnie Gintis, Joseph Kramer, and by everyone at the Gay Spirit Visions Conference, where the earliest stories were read. And Ron Lambe, Peter Kendrick, Rocco Patt, John Stowe, Monty Schuth, King Thackston, Jay Beard, Franklin Abbott, Gary Kaupman, Brian Helder whose wonderful film "Voices From The Sixth World" documents our tribal history, and Randy Taylor who copied and sent me Raven's images. Also Harry Hay and John Burnside, James Broughton and Joel Singer. And Dandelion, Al Cotton, Martin Isginitis, Gary Plouff, Dennis Van Avery, Duncan Teague, Tom Spanbauer, David-Michael Searcy, Dave MacDonald, Peter Bear Walks, Steve Palmer, Don Shewey, Nelson Bloncourt, Jeff Wadlington, Hawkins Mitchell, Mark Walker, Mark Thompson, Mark Honaker, John Fletcher Harris, Samuel Kirschner, John Pasqualetti, Danny Pietryk, Daniel Rothenfeld, Kerry Blasdel, Moses Mann, Tom Crow, Johannes Muller, Michel Schummer, Martin Raffael Siems, Manfred Ibel, Andrew Kelm, Philip Hare, Michael Pearl. Plus Arrasu, S, Altus, and all the angels in my life.

For "Poems for Our Tribe"

I want to thank everyone who came to the Winter Meditation held on Zoom by the Gay Spirit Visions Conference in January of 2021. GSV has been my spiritual home since the very first gathering in 1990. It was there that Harry Hay blessed me as a younger elder of our tribe, and GSV shaped my life and inspired many of these poems, a few of which I first read there. My time there also prepared me to be the older elder I am now, all these years later. I also want to thank the many men I met there over the years, some of whom have become beloved friends, and thank Don Shewey, Jonathan Lerner, and Franklin Abbott, whose own work as writers continues to inspire me. With gratitude to David Cable, Randy Taylor, Sequoia Lundy, Hunter Flournoy for their grounded wisdom. And some dancing partners over the decades – Bernd Larisch, Richard Krawetz, Denny Lyden, David Gitomer, Roger Lax, Edward Doty, Doug Guevara, Lenny Lubin, Lance Paavola, Rob Bernardo, Joseph McKay, Tony Losi, Gerard Rizza, Neil Weinberg, Mark Honaker, Stuart Schear, Moses Mann, Poonie Dodson, Ronnie Moseberth, Donald Coté, Randy Higgins, King Thackston, Darren Goldstein. And my wonderful blessing of a backup crew: some in and some out of bodies – Richard Ramer, Eileen Gordon, Traci Brown, Cindy Levinson, Steve Zipperstein, Michael Friedman, Marc Weinberger, Cheryl Woodruff, Lynne Reynolds, Ellen Melamed, Carol Robin, Bonnie Gintis, Alma Daniel, Lyssa Menard, David-Michael Searcy-Ramer, John Myers, Jasminder Kaur, Patanjali Venkatacharya, Harvey Schwartz, Jim Van Buskirk, Sara Felder, Dev Noily, Jesse Noily, Andréa Guerra, Sue Bojdak, Ruth Haber, Randy Furash-Stewart, Leo Hill, Sheri Hostetler, Kinari Webb, Stephanie Stevens, Aysha Hidayatullah, Levi Ramer, Hunter Flournoy, Niku Shah, Carey Averbook. And all of my muses, embodied and in spirit.

"The Temple of Father Earth and Mother Sky" was written many years ago for Steve Palmer. Thank you for opening the door to its contents.

"Father Earth Triptych" was written for and read at the Gay Spirit Visions Conference on Friday the 15th of September 2006.

"Wingsong" was written in 2004 in memory of my dear friend King Thackston, and for the friends and lovers who died of AIDS, some of whose names appear above.

"The Song of Father Earth" was written for him on the 19th of April in 2020.

"Ritual for Walks-Between Gatherings," is an adaptation of "Declaration on the Role of Gay Men in the World" which I wrote in 2002 for a GSV gathering.

With gratitude, I thank my ancestors and my dream self for the stories that gave birth to "When I Died."

Acknowledgments

*For everyone at Wipf and Stock
who worked on this book*

Matt Wimer, Managing Editor
Jason Robeck, Rights and Permissions
George Callihan, Editorial Assistant
Emily Callihan, Assistant Managing Editor
Kara Barlow, Endorsements Manager
Jonathan Hill, Typesetter
Shannon Carter, Designer

With deep gratitude!

Author Bio

IN ADDITION TO *Two Flutes Playing*, **Andrew Ramer** is the author of *Revelations for a New Millennium, Angel Answers, Queering the Text, Torah Told Different, Deathless,* and *Fragments of the Brooklyn Talmud.* He's a co-author of *The Spiritual Dimensions of Healing Addictions, Further Dimensions of Healing Addictions,* and the international best seller *Ask Your Angels.* An interview with him appears in *Gay Soul* by Mark Thompson, who interviewed and photographed sixteen gay writers, teachers, healers, and visionaries.

An ordained maggid (sacred storyteller in the Jewish tradition) Ramer was born in 1951 in Elm/hurst, New York, across the street from an amusement park called Fairyland, and now lives in Oak/land, California, up the street from an amusement park called Fairyland.

For more information you can visit his website: andrewramer. com

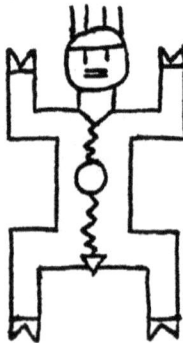